T0339561

Cambridge Elements ≡

Elements in Phonetics
edited by
David Deterding
Universiti Brunei Darussalam

PHONETICS IN LANGUAGE TEACHING

Di Liu
Temple University

Tamara Jones
Howard Community College

Marnie Reed
Boston University

CAMBRIDGE
UNIVERSITY PRESS

Shaftesbury Road, Cambridge CB2 8EA, United Kingdom

One Liberty Plaza, 20th Floor, New York, NY 10006, USA

477 Williamstown Road, Port Melbourne, VIC 3207, Australia

314–321, 3rd Floor, Plot 3, Splendor Forum, Jasola District Centre, New Delhi – 110025, India

103 Penang Road, #05–06/07, Visioncrest Commercial, Singapore 238467

Cambridge University Press is part of Cambridge University Press & Assessment, a department of the University of Cambridge.

We share the University's mission to contribute to society through the pursuit of education, learning and research at the highest international levels of excellence.

www.cambridge.org
Information on this title: www.cambridge.org/9781108994354

DOI: 10.1017/9781108992015

First published 2022

A catalogue record for this publication is available from the British Library.

ISBN 978-1-108-99435-4 Paperback
ISSN 2634-1689 (online)
ISSN 2634-1670 (print)

Phonetics in Language Teaching

Elements in Phonetics

DOI: 10.1017/9781108992015
First published online: December 2022

Di Liu
Temple University

Tamara Jones
Howard Community College

Marnie Reed
Boston University

Author for correspondence: Tamara Jones, tjones@howardcc.edu

Abstract: This Element explores ways in which language teachers, especially teachers of English, can benefit from knowledge of phonetics. It also offers recommendations for introducing and improving pronunciation teaching in the classroom. While hoping that this Element is useful to instructors of all languages, the majority of the examples come from North American English (NAE) and the English language classroom. At the same time, the Element acknowledges that English language teaching is rather different from the teaching of other languages, since today most interactions around the world in English do not involve a native speaker and use of English as a lingua franca (ELF) has become widespread. Teachers of English should be aware that their students may not want to mimic all aspects of native-speaker pronunciation, since some native-speaker patterns of speech, such as the extensive simplification and omission of sounds, may not be helpful in enhancing intelligibility.

This Element also has a video abstract: www.cambridge.org/
Phonetics_Jones_abstract

Keywords: phonetics, phonology, language teaching, listening, speaking, and pronunciation, second language acquisition

ISBNs: 9781108994354 (PB), 9781108992015 (OC)
ISSNs: 2634-1689 (online), 2634-1670 (print)

Contents

1 Introduction

Phonetics can be defined as the science which studies the characteristics of human speech and provides methods for their description, classification, and transcription (Crystal, 2003, p. 349). Of course, a detailed description of the production of speech is immensely complex: speech involves, for example, the coordination of over eighty different muscles (Laver, 1994, p. 1); furthermore, a comprehensive understanding of phonetics involves a wide range of different disciplines (Laver, 1994, p. 2). Indeed, scientific research on phonetics can involve many different techniques such as magnetic resonance imaging (MRI) and electropalatography (EPG) (Stone, 2010), and even introductory texts on phonetics tend to now make extensive reference to the acoustic analysis of speech (e.g. Ladefoged & Johnson, 2011), the interpretation of which can be quite technical.

This Element explores ways in which language teachers, especially teachers of English, can benefit from knowledge of phonetics. Language teachers do not need a detailed knowledge of all aspects of scientific research into phonetics or an extensive understanding of acoustics; but we assert that a basic understanding of the production of speech sounds, knowledge about how they can be described, and skills in their transcription are essential tools for the proficient language teacher. This Element provides an overview of this knowledge and these skills. We also offer recommendations for introducing pronunciation teaching in the classroom, and we hope that teachers will find some of these suggestions helpful.

In this Element, we connect phonetic knowledge and language teaching with the aim of providing an overview of phonetics that can be invaluable for teachers. Phonetic knowledge is closely related to multiple language skills including listening, speaking, and pronunciation. In particular, the study of phonetics covers all aspects of pronunciation teaching, which, in the past had what has been described as a "Cinderella status," being denied a proper role in language teaching despite the crucial importance of the work it does (Levis, 2018, p. 217). This Element thus focuses on how the status of pronunciation teaching can be improved, so that teachers and their students can make use of knowledge about and skills in the description, classification, and transcription of spoken language. We focus in Section 2 on phonetic transcription using the International Phonetic Alphabet (IPA), a skill which we believe is exceptionally valuable for language teachers and learners. In Section 3, we discuss the segmental articulation of consonants and vowels. Section 4 deals with consonants and vowels in context and connected speech processes (CSPs). Section 5 focuses on prosody, and Section 6 considers the state of the art including models of language teaching and use of computers to contribute to the teaching of listening, speaking, and pronunciation.

While we hope that this Element is useful to instructors of all languages, the majority of the examples will come from North American English (NAE) and the English language classroom, because English is the language that most readers will be familiar with and also because there is an extensive range of research on the pronunciation of English for teachers (e.g. Brown, 1991; Jones, 2016; Kang et al., 2018; Reed & Levis, 2015). Furthermore, focusing on English allows us to provide a substantial overview of aspects of the phonetics of the language, such as its transcription and articulation. At the same time, we acknowledge that English language teaching is rather different from the teaching of other languages in one important respect: nowadays, most interactions around the world in English do not involve a native speaker, and use of English as a lingua franca (ELF) – which can be defined as English used as the language of choice between speakers who do not share a common first language (Seidlhofer, 2011, p. 7) – has become widespread. When a speaker from Brazil is talking to someone from Japan using English, they are principally concerned about being understood and usually do not care very much how closely their pronunciation is aligned with native-speaker norms of speech (Jenkins, 2007). While knowledge about pronunciation is invaluable for language teachers and their pupils, teachers of English should be aware that their students may not want to mimic all aspects of native-speaker pronunciation; and indeed, some native-speaker patterns of speech, such as the extensive simplification and omission of sounds that will be discussed in Section 4.5, may not be helpful in enhancing intelligibility. We consider the issue of intelligibility further in Section 1.1 before we discuss some models of learning pronunciation in Section 1.2, offer a brief overview of approaches to language teaching in Section 1.3, and then summarize the role of phonetics in language teaching in Section 1.4.

1.1 The Intelligibility Principle

In the past, learning a foreign language usually involved closely imitating the speech patterns of native speakers. For learning English, this raises the issue of which native speakers should be imitated. Speakers of NAE? Or speakers of standard southern British English (SSBE), the standard model of British English, which was formerly called received pronunciation and is also sometimes referred to as BBC English (Roach, 2009)? Or maybe another accent, such as that of Australia?

Quite apart from the selection of a pronunciation model, we should note that after the age of about twelve, it is difficult for most learners to develop native-like pronunciation (Abrahamsson & Hyltenstam, 2009). Furthermore, we should acknowledge that many learners of English, particularly those in ELF contexts, want to communicate effectively using the language without trying to pretend that they come from the USA, the UK, or Australia (Jenkins, 2007). In other words, they are concerned with achieving a high level of intelligibility, and closely mimicking a native-speaker model is not necessarily the most effective way of achieving this.

Before we discuss the implications for teaching pronunciation, we consider what is meant by the concepts of intelligibility, comprehensibility, and accentedness. Derwing and Munro (2005) have suggested definitions differentiating these three concepts, as summarized in Table 1.

Table 1 Definitions of intelligibility, comprehensibility, and accentedness

Concepts	Definition
Intelligibility	the extent to which a listener actually understands an utterance
Comprehensibility	a listener's perception of how difficult it is to understand an utterance
Accentedness	a listener's perception of how different a speaker's accent is from that of the local L1 community

The intelligibility principle holds that the goal of pronunciation teaching and learning is intelligible speech, regardless of how native-like it sounds (Derwing & Munro, 2015, p. 6), and most current pronunciation instruction strives for the practical goal of a high level of intelligibility, that is learners producing speech that can be understood by a range of different listeners. Comprehensibility is also crucial, as it is important not just to be understood but also to be easily understood, but accentedness is less important for many students. For the overwhelming majority of learners of English, close imitation of native-speech accents is not important, while being easily understood by people around the world is.

At the same time, however, there certainly are some learners who do want to try to fully integrate into a native-speaker society, and for them, close imitation of the local patterns of speech may be important. "Even if people can understand what [a speaker is] saying, an off-target pronunciation may still sound *comical*, *irritating*, or *distracting* to listeners" (Carley & Mees, 2021, p. 1). For those who are not trying to integrate into a native-speaker society, it is important to ensure that their pronunciation is not comical or irritating, so they need to ensure that their accent is not a distraction. Teachers need to evaluate the priorities and aspirations of their students and adjust their teaching appropriately.

Quite apart from this evaluation of the needs and aspirations of learners, a key issue for teachers involves determining which aspects of pronunciation contribute most to enhancing intelligibility, and this is an ongoing research issue (Deterding, 2013; Pickering, 2006). Many language educators and researchers refer to the segmentals – the consonant and vowel sounds – as the building blocks for larger units, such as syllables, words, and phrases (Rogerson-Revell, 2018, p. 93). When students do not have a strong grasp of these building blocks, their ability to speak in the target language is severely impaired. In addition to consonants and vowels, language teachers and learners need to consider suprasegmental features, those features that extend beyond individual segments, including stress, rhythm, and intonation. The relative contribution of segmentals and suprasegmentals to improvement in intelligibility remains a topic of discussion, but it is generally agreed that both areas are important (McNerney & Mendelsohn,1992; Zielinski, 2015).

Jenkins (2000) investigated the relative importance of various features of pronunciation. She proposed a lingua franca core (LFC), an inventory of those features of pronunciation that are important for international intelligibility, and she suggests that noncore features do not need to be taught. Included in the LFC are all the consonants of English apart from /θ/ and /ð/ (the sounds at the start of *think* and *that* respectively), word-initial and medial consonant clusters, the distinction between tense and lax vowels (also often referred to as long and short vowels), and sentence stress; noncore features include /θ/ and /ð/, vowel quality (e.g. the exact distinction in vowel height of different vowels), the weak forms of function words, stress-timed rhythm, and the specific tunes associated with intonation (Jenkins, 2000, pp. 23–24). Many of these, such as the exclusion of vowel quality, remain controversial. Issues related to segments will be discussed further in Sections 3 and 4 of this Element, while rhythm and intonation will be covered in Section 5.

Even though the exact features of the LFC are subject to ongoing research, the concept that achieving a high level of intelligibility is key for learners of a language is a well-established principle of language teaching. One other key concept is the distinction between perception and production: while many learners of English may not aspire to imitate native-speaker patterns closely, they do need to be able to understand those patterns. In practical terms, they do not have to adopt all the features associated with fast, fluent utterances produced by native speakers, including assimilation, simplification, and omission of sounds, but they must be able to understand speech that includes that kind of speech. This will be discussed further in Section 4.5.

1.2 Models of Speech Learning

Here we briefly discuss three models which relate the potential for accurate perception and production of new sounds, or phones, to the degree of similarity between L1 and L2 sounds: the contrastive analysis hypothesis (CAH) originally proposed by Lado (1957); the speech learning model (SLM) suggested by Flege (1995), and the perceptual assimilation model (PAM) developed by Best (1995).

The CAH was an extension of contrastive analysis (CA), a comparative linguistics methodology utilizing structural linguistics to predict error that sought to establish similarities and differences between languages as a basis for improving foreign language instruction. Adapting the CA approach to a focus on predicting learner difficulty, Lado (1957) formulated the CAH which, in its strong form, attempted to predict (a priori) which features learners will find difficult to acquire, starting with pronunciation of sounds. The CAH is based on a comparison between the native and target language, under the assumption that similar "elements" will be easy whereas those that differ will be difficult. Specifically, it was predicted that L2 phonemes with no L1 counterpart would be difficult to learn, while equivalent L1-L2 phonemes would be relatively easy to learn. Although intended to account for learner difficulty, in actual practice the CAH, as with all prevailing CA approaches, was used to predict errors, perhaps on the unconscious assumption that difficulty and error can be equated. It was also wrongly assumed that pronunciation errors resulted from faulty production, that is incorrect articulation of the speech sound, as opposed to faulty perception. This approach also failed to take into account that while two languages may share the same sound, that phoneme may differ at the phonetic level, that is in how it is articulated depending on its phonological environment. To illustrate, consider the voiceless phonemes /p/, /t/, and /k/, referred to as stop consonants or plosives because their bilabial, alveolar, or velar place of articulation stops the airflow from the lungs. In English, these phonemes, when released in word-initial or stressed syllable-initial position, are accompanied by a burst of air referred to as aspiration. The resulting conditioned variants or allophones – aspirated [p^h], [t^h], or [k^h] – occur in predictable phonological environments in English but do not occur in these positions in other languages, such as Spanish, which share the same sounds at the phonemic level. Further, the CA approach overlooked individual differences, including among learners with a shared L1 at comparable levels of proficiency. Failure to take into account crosslinguistic differences in the allophonic distribution of the "same" phonemes at the phonetic level or to recognize the role of conditioned variants of phonemes in L1 acquisition, along with evidence that not all predicted errors occur and that not all speakers of a particular L1 make the same errors in their L2 speech all combined to weaken the strong form of the CAH. As empirical evidence failed to support the major claims of the hypothesis, particularly that the closer the target phone is to an L1 category the easier it is to perceive and produce, the CAH eventually fell out of favor.

The SLM (Flege, 1995) addresses a major failure of CA to account for L2 speech learning, namely reliance on phoneme inventories without respect to phonetic realization, that is positional allophonic variation of the phonemes. The SLM, a model of the influence of the L1 on L2 speech learning, also takes issue with the critical period hypothesis, which presumed discontinuity in postpuberty language learning ability (Lenneberg, 1967). Assuming instead that phonetic category formation is not age limited, the SLM addresses how phonetic systems reorganize over the life span and whether highly experienced L2 learners will eventually "master" L2 sounds. It stipulates which L2 sounds are most challenging to perceive and produce on the basis of equivalence classification. The SLM claims that similar but not identical sounds are perceived as instances of L1 sounds through a subconscious cognitive mechanism of interlingual identification, and that this perceptual linking to L1 sounds initially forestalls establishment of new phonetic categories. Flege's model, which concerns the requisite mental representation for perceiving new target sounds, accounts for early stage nontarget realization of new L2 sounds; that is the degree of accuracy with which L2 segments are perceived establishes and constrains the degree of accuracy with which they can be produced. The greater the perceived dissimilarity or distance between the L1 sound and a target sound, the more readily learners will establish a new target-like category. Proposing a perceptual basis for production errors challenges the assumption that we lose neurocognitive plasticity by suggesting eventual category and motoric implementation alignment for some, though not necessarily all L2 sounds that differ audibly from the closest L1 sound.

The SLM accounts for improved discrimination as the result of phonetic category formation, considered essential for phonetic reorganization, claiming "the processes and mechanisms used in learning the L1 sound system, including category formation, remain intact over the life-span and can be applied to L2 learning" (Best & Tyler, 2007, p. 24). Retention of speech-learning capacity allows L2 learners to "gradually discern" phonetic differences between close but not identical sounds – described by SLM as a slow process, but one that is sensitive to phonetic input during L2 learning.

In its revised formulation (Flege & Bohn, 2021), the SLM-r adjusts its focus from eventual mastery or ultimate attainment to L2 speech development across the life span, with no presumed end state, consistent with L1 speech-development literature. SLM-r considers it unproductive and no longer of theoretical interest to determine whether or the extent to which an L2 learner's speech perception or production is distinguishable from that of a native speaker. Further, whereas the SLM focused on between-group differences, for example highly experienced versus inexperienced L2 learners or child versus adult learners, SLM-r focuses on individual differences, with emphasis on factors such as the quality and quantity of input L2 learners receive, learners' auditory acuity, and working auditory memory. It acknowledges that the frequency of target language use is a stronger predictor of foreign accent than critical period effects. Moreover, where the original SLM looked broadly at the factors chronological age at first exposure to an L2 and length of residence, SLM-r more deeply considers how precisely developed the learner's L1 phonetic categories are at time of first L2 exposure. The L1 category precision assumption states that the more precisely defined L1 categories are, the more readily differences between an L1 sound and the closest L2 sound will be detected, allowing for a new phonetic category to be formed. With respect to interactions between perception and production, the former unidirectional claim that accurate L2 segmental perception constrains L2 speech production has been replaced by a "co-evolution" hypothesis on the basis of empirical evidence supporting a bidirectional relationship between perception and production. With these and other refinements, the SLM-r seeks to continue the investigation into how speech is learned across the life span while taking into account individual differences in L2 attainment.

The PAM, an articulatory framework developed by Best (1995), examined the role of the native language in shaping consonant and vowel perception. The focus of this model is the mechanism by which learners' perceptual systems attempt to match, or assimilate, new or unfamiliar speech sounds to known or established L1 categories. The PAM draws information on how native phonological categories develop from research in infant speech perception. Native perceptual systems develop in correspondence with the inventory of L1 sounds, with discriminatory ability for sounds that are not in the L1 input gradually diminishing between the ages of eight to twelve months, a phenomenon known as perceptual narrowing (Werker & Tees, 1983). Native categories are established on the basis of contrast between phonemes, the consonant and vowel building blocks of languages, such that the English consonant phonemes /t/ and /d/ are separate categories, capable of creating minimal-pair distinctions, for example *to*/*do* or *bat*/*bad.* Native speakers tend not to discriminate consonants from within a single category, as when native speakers of English hear allophones (phonologically conditioned variants) of the phoneme /t/, for example the glottal stop in words like *kitten* or the flap in words like *water*, as one sound, /t/.

The PAM draws on research in cross-language speech perception to determine the potential of adult L2 learners to discriminate nonnative contrasts. The model predicts that accurate perceptual discrimination of previously unheard nonnative sounds, or phones, depends on whether and to what degree they are assimilated to native phonological categories. Whether pairs of phonologically contrasting never-before-heard nonnative phones will be assimilated depends on whether the listener can detect a native phonological distinction between the nonnative phones. Best (1995) established empirically what types of phoneme contrasts are easy for L2 learning and which pose challenges. A good discrimination is predicted if an L1 phonological contrast is detected between contrasting nonnative phones, such that each of the pair assimilates to a different L1 phonological category, a two-category assimilation. A poor discrimination is predicted in the case where no difference is detected between two nonnative phones, which then map onto one L1 phone, a single-category assimilation.

Having attributed differences to the ways nonnative sounds align with gestural constellations of native phonological categories, PAM related disparities in perception of foreign contrasts to disparities in native phonological knowledge gained through linguistic experience. Building upon PAM, PAM-L2 (Best & Tyler, 2007) expanded the scope of perceptual learning to encompass the role of attentional focus in detecting phonological contrasts as a basis for forming a new L2 category. Ability to detect a phonetic difference between contrasting L2 phonemes is claimed to facilitate perceptual learning.

To illustrate the challenges of perceiving and then producing unfamiliar speech sounds as modeled by PAM, consider the following case of a student from Venezuela. During self-introductions in a L2 classroom, he used /β/, a voiced bilabial fricative that exists in his native language Spanish, but not in English. To an English native speaker, this rendered his native country sounding like "Benezuela" and his profession sounding like "diborce" attorney. The Spanish phoneme shares two features with the English target /v/ phoneme: the fricative manner of articulation, and voicing; but it shares bilabial place of articulation with the perceived phoneme /b/, instead of the expected labiodental place of articulation for /v/. Granting that pronunciation of country names can be regarded as the purview of the native speaker, the problematic pronunciation of his profession by this English-language learner may be more worthy of attention from the English as a second language (ESL) instructor.

Because naive English-speaking listeners with whom this student expects to interact will perceptually associate /β/ with the closest English phoneme /b/, and cognizant that self-introductions provide just one chance to make a good first impression, it can be argued that the student would benefit from explicit instruction focused on the place of articulation of /v/.

1.3 Phonetics in Language Teaching

Language teaching has a long history and has adopted various methods, including the grammar-translation method, which involved substantial knowledge of grammar and was based on translation from the source language to the target language, and the audiolingual method, which depended on extensive use of recordings in language laboratories in the belief that multiple repetition of words led to perfection in their production. More recently, communicative language teaching (CLT) became the dominant approach; it advocates a focus on the use of language for purposes of genuine interpersonal communication.

In each of these methods, phonetic skills had a different status. The grammar-translation method was mostly focused on written texts; phonetic skills were not regarded as important. In contrast, phonetic skills were central in the audiolingual method. In CLT, explicit pronunciation instruction is often given a less prominent role, in the belief that phonetic accuracy is not essential for communication of the message. However, many people now believe that the exclusion of phonetics knowledge from the language teaching curriculum is misguided, as it has been shown that unexpected pronunciation, even in ELF contexts, is the factor that most often leads to a loss of intelligibility and a breakdown in communication (Deterding, 2013).

Phonetics in language teaching is both an art and a science. It is an art because it is creative, adaptive, and innovative in its nature. Phonetics in language teaching often involves creative adaptation of teaching materials according to different instructional contexts and settings; consideration of learners' objectives, age, proficiency levels, motivations, aspirations, and many other factors; and application of innovative and emerging technology that can be used imaginatively to enhance language teaching. As a science, it requires interdisciplinary knowledge, for in order to teach listening, speaking, and pronunciation effectively, instructors need to have content knowledge about phonetics, background knowledge about second-language development, and pedagogical knowledge about language teaching. They need to be able to identify, transcribe, and describe sounds based on phonetic knowledge, to select optimal teaching approaches based on an understanding of second language development, and to design effective teaching methods based on their experience of language teaching.

Clearly, phonetics benefits language learners, even in CLT-based classrooms, when they are provided with instruction in and practice with the description and classification of sounds and the perception and production of target-language phonemes. Unfortunately, a number of studies report that many educators, including English language-teaching professionals, receive insufficient training in pronunciation teaching, so they feel ill-prepared to deal with it in the classroom (Baker, 2014; Foote et al., 2011; Murphy, 2014). Even those who have received some training in phonetics often rely on their own intuition when conveying the concepts to language learners (Levis, 2005), which may initially result in teacher-centered pronunciation instruction with limited communicative application (Burri & Baker, 2021). The gaps in knowledge affect all areas of phonetics, a topic which many teachers find daunting (Couper, 2017, p. 830), with the result that many feel that it is simply too difficult for them to teach pronunciation (Zielinski & Yates, 2014, p. 57).

Fortunately, when language teachers feel empowered to teach pronunciation, explicit instruction in the articulation of target-language phonemes has the potential to make a substantial difference in students' intelligibility (Couper, 2006).

Educators often report a desire for practical tips and techniques that will help them introduce target-language sounds. As a result, this Element attempts to bridge the divide between what language teachers may already know about teaching phonetics and what they need to know in order to provide the most effective pronunciation instruction to their students. It also offers some ideas about how skills in pronunciation can help their students. Specifically, the following aspects are discussed:

1. Sounds are abstract and transient in nature. To teach sounds and to provide feedback to students, teachers need to be able to describe sounds. Crucially, accurate description of sounds involves transcription, and we deal with this in Section 2.

2. Learners need to know how phonemes in the target language are similar to and different from those in their first languages (Best et al., 2001; Vihman, 1993). Further, learners benefit from understanding how the positioning and use of speech organs affect the production of sounds (Howard & Messum, 2011; Mompean, 2003). Issues related to the description and articulation of phonemes are addressed in Section 3.

3. Learners need to know how sounds can change when they occur in close proximity to other sounds in a stream of speech (Lowie & Bultena, 2007). Sounds do not occur in isolation, and they vary depending on where they occur. Furthermore, they can undergo substantial change

when produced in fluent speech. These areas are considered in greater detail in Section 4.

4. The study of prosody includes rhythm (the regular occurrence in time of a unit of speech) and intonation (the tunes associated with utterances), and learners should be familiar with these areas of phonetics and how they affect the intelligibility of their speech. This is discussed in Section 5.

5. Finally, there are many computer-based tools that can enhance pronunciation teaching, and all language learners can benefit from these. In Section 6 we review some resources for pronunciation teaching that can be usefully introduced in the language classroom.

2 Phonetic Transcription

Before we discuss the symbols and systems used for phonetic transcription, we would like to first invite you to a language class that took place several years ago in an institute in the United States. This is a case that demonstrates how some teachers integrate phonetic transcription in language teaching. The setting was an English for Academic Purposes class, and the students were high-intermediate adult learners who were preparing to study in a US university. The teacher had been working in the language institution for many years and the classes she taught included listening, speaking, and integrated skills classes.

At the beginning of the class, the teacher wrote some IPA symbols on the whiteboard and asked students to describe those symbols using three parameters she had introduced in the previous class to represent consonants: voicing, place of articulation, and manner of articulation. She produced these sounds, one at a time, and asked her students to repeat after her. Then, she gave out some practice exercises and asked students to transcribe them using IPA symbols and provide a phonetic description of their articulation. Although students were able to complete the transcription exercise, they did not enjoy the activity. Also, students mispronounced sounds in the following classes despite successfully completing the transcription activities.

This example raises two questions:

1. Do we need a set of symbols to describe and transcribe sounds?
2. Does successful description and transcription of sounds lead to correct production?

To answer the first question, we review the development of phonetic transcription. In later sections, we describe approaches that can help address the second question.

2.1 The Role of Phonetic Transcription in Language Teaching

One essential aspect of phonetics for language teaching is the knowledge of phonetic transcription. Unlike spelling, phonetic transcription uses symbols that match each sound to a unique symbol so that reading the symbols shows the teacher and learners the actual pronunciation of a word or phrase. Knowledge of phonetic transcription is a critical content skill for language teachers, and such knowledge helps them to identify how words are pronounced in the target language and how their learners are missing the mark in their own pronunciation. Furthermore, it can be helpful in explaining how to make new sounds.

One widely used system of transcription involves the IPA, which was originally developed in 1889 with the intention of describing the sounds of all the world's languages and has remained remarkably consistent since then (Esling, 2010). At its most basic, the IPA can be used to represent the sounds of consonants in terms of their voicing, place, and manner of articulation, and to represent vowels in terms of lip rounding and the height and position of the tongue (IPA, 1999). These ways of describing the pronunciation of consonants and vowels will be adopted in Section 3 of this Element.

The convention for representing the phonemes of a language – the meaningful units that differentiate sounds in the language – is to enclose them in slashes: a broad transcription. For example, English has three voiceless plosive consonant phonemes – /p, t, k/ – which are produced with no vocal cord vibration and are often referred to as stops because they briefly stop the airflow. These phonemes vary in their articulation according to their phonological context, and these variants, known as allophones, are represented in square brackets: a narrow transcription. For instance, while the phoneme /p/ appears in both *pit* and *spit*, the pronunciation differs slightly: while the /p/ in the initial position in *pit* is released with an accompanying puff of air, known as aspiration, there is no aspiration associated with the /p/ in *spit* because of the influence of the fricative /s/ at the start of the word. The aspirated and unaspirated allophones of /p/ are represented as [pʰ] and [p] respectively.

One reason for the crucial need for a system of transcription such as the IPA is the mismatch between spelling and sound in any language. In languages like Spanish, the mismatch is smaller and the pronunciation is relatively predictable from the spelling. In a language like English, the mismatch is very noticeable. English letters may correspond to multiple sounds; for example the letter <a> is pronounced differently in *apple, father, walk*, and *about*. Using IPA transcription, these vowel sounds are shown as /æ, ɑ, ɔ, ə/ respectively. Because there are only five vowel letters in English, the written system is insufficient to show the range of vowel sounds in the language. In addition, different letters in English may represent the same sound: the letters <c> in *cat* and <k> in *kitten* are pronounced with the same sound, and the letter <f> in *fish* and the letter combination <ph> in *Phillip* similarly have the same sound. Using IPA transcription, the same sound is always transcribed using a consistent symbol, so the sound at the start of *cat* and *kitten* is shown as /k/ and that at the start of *fish* and *Phillip* is /f/.

When instructors are teaching and explaining pronunciation to language learners, it is difficult to refer to different sounds properly without a systematic transcription system such as the IPA. There are several issues that make learning the IPA, or a similar phonetic transcription system, beneficial.

1. Phonemes and allophones usually differ substantially between the first language of learners and the language they are learning (Levis, 1999, p. 65). For instance, Mandarin Chinese has the voiceless palatal fricative /ɕ/ at the start of words such as 西, *xī* (west), Spanish has the voiceless velar fricative /x/ in the middle of words such as *ojo* (eye) and French has the voiced uvular fricative /ʁ/ at the start of *rouge* (red) but none of these sounds occur in English. Use of the IPA enables students to appreciate differences between the sounds of their languages and the target language.

2. Learners cannot easily perceive sounds that do not exist in their L1 sound inventories. For example, Mandarin Chinese does not have the voiceless dental fricative (Duanmu, 2007), the sound which is transcribed as /θ/ and occurs at the start of *thank*, and so learners of English in China may use /s/ in place of /θ/, producing *sank you* instead of *thank you* (Deterding, 2006). Some Chinese learners of English find it challenging to discriminate between /s/ and /θ/, and use of IPA transcription helps highlight this distinction.

3. The transient nature of speech and limited time available for classroom instruction leads to few classroom practice opportunities. In the classroom, a teacher may try to elicit a target sound production from a student by modeling it, and sometimes, after multiple attempts, either the student ends up producing the right sound accidentally or the instructor simply gives up because there is not enough time in the lesson to ensure the student can hear and produce the sound accurately. Use of the IPA can help fix sounds in the memory of students.

2.2 Phonetic Transcription and Notation in Textbooks

Although the IPA has a long and consistent history (Esling, 2010), it is not the only transcription system. In the field of language teaching, there are variations in the system and symbols used in different textbooks and resources. For example, one of the most widely used coursebooks for teachers of NAE, Celce-Murcia et al. (2010), sometimes deviates from the IPA. For instance, the IPA symbol /y/ represents a front rounded vowel (the vowel which occurs in *tu*, "you," in French and is represented as <ü> both in German words such as *über*, "over," and in the Pinyin system for Mandarin Chinese, as in 女, *nǚ*, [woman]), but Celce-Murcia et al. (2010) use /y/ for the sound at the start of words such as *yes*. Table 2 shows some of the different symbols that are used in the IPA and three pronunciation teaching textbooks. The first two, Celce-Murcia et al. (2010) and Gilbert (2012), present American English while Roach (2009) deals with SSBE (though he refers to it as "BBC pronunciation"). Symbols not shown in Table 2 are generally consistently used in the IPA and in various textbooks.

Table 2 Different symbols used in the IPA and three textbooks

Sample Words	IPA	Celce-Murcia et al. (2010)	Gilbert (2012)	Roach (2009)
yes	/j/	/y/	/y/	/j/
cake, pay	/eɪ/	/ey/	/eʸ/	/eɪ/
tea, key	/i/	/iy/	/iʸ/	/iː/
ice, pie	/aɪ/	/ay/	/aʸ/	/aɪ/
road, know	/oʊ/	/ow/	/oʷ/	/əʊ/
blue, school	/u/	/uw/	/uʷ/	/uː/
house, cow	/aʊ/	/aw/	/aʷ/	/aʊ/
boy, join	/ɔɪ/	/ɔy/	/ɔʸ/	/ɔɪ/

Given these differences, teachers naturally will have questions about which transcription system they should use; thus, we need to address the following two issues:

1. What are the sources of the IPA symbols?
2. Why do some textbook authors use alternative symbols?

Most IPA symbols originate from an extended Roman alphabet; a few, such as /θ/, are from the Greek alphabet; some symbols, such as /ɪ/ (the vowel in *kit*), are modified versions of Roman letters; and finally, there are symbols derived from more specialized alphabets, such as /ʃ/ (the sound at the start of *she*), which is like the integral symbol in mathematics (MacMahon, 1996, p. 823).

Because of the multiple origins of symbols, some will be more familiar to students than others. It is therefore important to point out that mastering a phonetic transcription system is not learning a whole new set of symbols of which the students have no prior knowledge. In fact, the majority of the symbols, like the initial consonants /b/, /d/, and /s/ in the words *boy, dance,* and *sing,* are likely to be familiar to learners and learning the symbols for these consonant sounds should be fairly straightforward for them. Symbols like /θ/ and /ʃ/ may be less familiar. The IPA relies on symbols such as these because, as mentioned above, there are not enough letters in the Roman alphabet for all the sounds in the languages of the world. As every symbol should uniquely represent one sound, new symbols must be introduced. Table 3 shows some of the non-Roman symbols and sample words:

Table 3 Sample non-Roman symbols in the IPA

Consonants	Sample Words	Vowels	Sample Words
/θ/	**thank, both**	/ɪ/	Sit
/ð/	**the, bathe**	/æ/	Bat
/ʃ/	**show, wash**	/ɔ/	Talk
/ʒ/	measure, beige	/ʌ/	But
/ʧ/	**choose, rich**	/ʊ/	Book
/dʒ/	**jump, bridge**	/ɝ/	herd
/ŋ/	**sink, sing**	/ə/	about

In an attempt to reduce the number of unfamiliar symbols, many textbook authors adopt alternatives to the IPA system. For example, English does not have the close front rounded vowel /y/. Thus, some textbook writers use /y/ instead of the IPA symbol /j/ to represent the sound at the start of words such as *yes.* In this case the phonetic symbol is the same as the letter, and the burden of memorizing an extra symbol due to a mismatch between letters and phonetic transcription has been reduced.

If we limit the scope to English, the modified textbook notation system is advantageous in that it is more straightforward and requires less time and effort to learn. However, it is useful for teachers to have familiarity with the IPA, as such knowledge allows them to refer to specific sounds in learners' L1s that may not exist in English. It is recommended that teachers make the selection of the transcription system they adopt based on their teaching contexts.

When implementing this decision, consistency is important because shifting between two systems will introduce discrepancies to the material, which many students already regard as complex. Teachers also need to be aware that students may have used a different system previously. Thus, knowing what transcription system(s) and symbols students already know before introducing the IPA is helpful. Finally, it is useful to develop a chart that places side by side the words, the symbols that are going to be used in the class, and any other symbols students may be familiar with.

2.3 Phonetic Transcription in Teacher Preparation and Language Classrooms

It has been reported that teachers receive insufficient training in phonetics and pronunciation teaching (Breitkreutz et al., 2001; Derwing & Munro, 2005). Recent years, though, have witnessed an increased coverage of these areas in teacher training programs (Foote et al., 2011). However, researchers have found that, despite widespread agreement that phonetic knowledge and transcription are useful, many educators lack interest in these areas. Furthermore, teachers have reported challenges when attempting to transfer phonetic knowledge into teaching practice, as they often lack confidence with use of the symbols (Couper, 2017).

Explicit phonetic instruction is effective in improving learners' pronunciation proficiency when it is adopted in classroom teaching, particularly in English as a foreign language (EFL) settings (Saito, 2007, 2012). There are two aspects involved in the classroom use of phonetic transcription. First, teachers need to explicitly teach the transcription system itself, including a set of symbols as discussed previously, as well as the parameters used to categorize and describe the articulation of the various sounds. Second, they need to integrate phonetic transcription with the use of the new language, adopting phonetic transcription when teaching new vocabulary to students and using phonetic knowledge when providing feedback on students' pronunciation errors. In Section 3, we will review the use of transcription in teaching activities and offer suggestions for approaches that teachers might adopt when raising awareness about articulation.

Crucial to the teaching of pronunciation is linking a transcription system such as the IPA to the articulation of sounds, including where and how they are produced. It is more important to explain to students how sounds are produced than to get them to memorize technical terms, for example that /b/ is a voiced bilabial plosive. As we discuss in Section 3, teachers may even develop a more learner-friendly terminology system for the places of articulation, for instance talking about the *lips* instead of *bilabial*.

With increased attention to the field of pronunciation teaching, several studies have been conducted to review practices and the effectiveness of methods of instruction, including read-aloud, drills, imitation, picture narratives, and spontaneous speaking (Lee et al., 2015; Saito, 2012; Thomson & Derwing, 2015). While phonetic transcription is not directly involved in most of these activities, it serves a fundamental role in that it increases learners' metalinguistic awareness of the sounds. It also offers a set of tools for teachers to distinguish between correct and incorrect pronunciation and provide feedback.

Incorporating IPA transcription practice into English lessons can be done fairly seamlessly. As students learn target phonemes, they can also learn the phonetic symbol for the sound. As a review activity, teachers can dictate words and have the students write them using the phonetic symbols. This can be transformed into a game by distributing pieces of paper and markers and encouraging pairs of students to race against other pairs to do the phonetic transcriptions quickly and accurately. Educators who want to infuse their lessons with some movement can create sets of matching index cards with words on half of the cards and the phonetic symbols on the other half, telling the students to mingle around the classroom and read the words on their cards until they find their match. If teachers want to help students practice the quick identification of a phoneme, they might write several phonetic symbols on the board and divide the class into teams, giving each team a different colored flyswatter. As they call out a word, students from each team race to hit the phonetic symbol for the initial sound of the word. Finally, of course, teachers can have their students phonetically transcribe new vocabulary as they learn it. This is perhaps the most useful practice for students because it helps them pronounce new words accurately.

2.4 Questions about Phonetic Transcription in Language Classrooms

We have reviewed the development, needs, purpose, and uses of a phonetic transcription system for segmental sounds. The use of such a system is beneficial in language classrooms. Here, we would like to address some common questions from preservice and in-service teachers with regard to the uses of phonetic transcription in classrooms.

Question 1: Can I teach English sounds without using the IPA or other transcription system?

It is important to adopt some kind of consistent phonetic transcription system, either the IPA or some other system. Phonetic transcription can be beneficial in two ways: 1. it helps learners to become aware that, in English, one sound can correspond to multiple spellings and one letter or letter combination can have different sounds; 2. when learners have difficulty discriminating two sounds, teachers can explicitly indicate the differences by using the phonetic symbols and parameters.

However, it is important to understand that teaching the IPA or a transcription of sounds does not necessarily lead to the improvement of learners' language skills. Some pronunciation-related instruction such as internalizing transcription conventions and understanding the articulatory or acoustic correlates of specific segmental and suprasegmental features of English are theoretical and not pedagogical in nature (Tsunemoto et al., 2020). While these activities may improve learners' explicit knowledge, they may not have a direct impact on learners' spontaneous production.

It is also important to point out that the same functions that teachers typically use IPA for can be achieved by using alternative tools such as the Color Vowel Chart (Taylor & Thompson, 2015) or phonics, which is commonly used for teaching reading to preschoolers (Ehri et al., 2001). Additionally, research shows that both phonetic symbols and keywords can be used to improve learners' perception, and the two techniques can be equally beneficial (Fouz-González & Mompean, 2021; Mompean & Fouz-González, 2021).

Question 2: Should I use broad or narrow transcription?

Broad transcription is usually sufficient, but narrow transcription may sometimes be helpful, because it provides details of the exact pronunciation of words. For example, as described earlier, to show the difference between two allophones such as the /p/ in *spit* and *pit*, we can show the first as [p] and the second as [pʰ].

The choice of broad versus narrow transcription depends on the purposes of teaching activities. Mompean (2017) suggests combining a broad phonemic transcription with narrow transcription of salient allophonic variants and/or CSPs for language teaching purposes. Using NAE, this would entail a basic broad transcription but with further detail for variants such as the glottal stop [ʔ] that can occur as an allophone of /t/ in words like *kitten*.

Question 3: I teach in an ELF setting – How does this affect the use of phonetic transcription in my class?

English as a lingua franca interactions involve speakers with different L1s using English to communicate (Seidlhofer, 2011, p. 7), and this contrasts with L2 contexts in which students are trying to integrate into a native-English society. The key in ELF settings is the enhancement of intelligibility, and mimicking native-speaker norms is not necessary in such contexts. However, it has also been shown that pronunciation is the source of most cases of misunderstanding in ELF contexts (Deterding, 2013), and reference to a transcription system such as the IPA is crucial in improving intelligibility.

At the same time, it may not be necessary to learn all the symbols or become familiar with all aspects of native-speaker pronunciation. Instructors of ELF may want to consider Jenkins' (2000) LFC, the inventory of those sounds that are necessary for maintaining international intelligibility in English. In such settings, teachers do not need to address details of pronunciation that are outside the LFC, such as the dark /l/ at the end of a word such as *pill* (which can be shown as [ɫ]).

Question 4: With limited time in class, which sound(s) should I prioritize?

The sounds to prioritize should depend on the functional load of the sounds and also the L1 background of the students. For classes involving students with a range of L1s, use of personalized training tools may be helpful.

Functional load estimates the importance of a phonetic contrast for communication by referring to the number of minimal pairs between two sounds (Brown, 1988). For instance, *berry*, /beri/, and *very*, /veri/, constitute a minimal pair because they are only distinguished by the two initial sounds /b/ and /v/. The functional load for /b/ and /v/ is quite high, because there are many minimal pairs for them, and it is vitally important that students differentiate between them. Simply put, "The most important sounds are the ones that can change the meaning of words" (Carley & Mees, 2021, p. 1).

It is also useful to consider learners' L1s when determining the sounds to focus on. For instance, if a teacher is teaching a class in which most students are Japanese English learners, then focusing on the contrast between /ɹ/ and /l/ (the sounds at the start of *right* and *light*) would be an effective strategy, because Japanese does not distinguish these sounds and Japanese learners of English often have problems with them.

In a class composed of students of various language backgrounds, however, instructors may want to leverage personalized training with technology. For example, they may provide high variability pronunciation training by using English Accent Coach (www.englishaccentcoach.com/) for perceptual training. They may also use apps like Sounds of Speech (https://soundsofspeech.uiowa.edu/) to visualize the use of speech organs and speech processes and help learners to establish connections between sounds, phonetic symbols, and the articulation processes.

3 Articulation of Segments

To help students become proficient in producing the phonemes of a language, it is valuable for instructors to be familiar with the anatomical and physical processes involved in forming them. Because of this, teaching the sound inventory is different from instruction on other aspects of a language.

Celce-Murcia et al. (2010, p. 43) note that, as pronunciation is a motor activity that involves sensory and physiological challenges, teachers can use tactile and kinesthetic methods to help their students master these challenges.

An important aspect of these approaches involves familiarity with the anatomy responsible for sound production – the *vocal tract*. In addition, educators need to understand how proficient speakers manipulate their speech organs to produce sounds. Finally, since teaching all of the phonemes and allophones of a language is an unreasonable expectation in most educational contexts, instructors also benefit from identifying which target-language sounds will prove the most challenging for their particular students and also which ones are the most important for them to learn to maximize their intelligibility.

One crucial aspect of a needs analysis involves determining if the learners want to try to approximate a native-speaker accent as nearly as possible, perhaps in order to assimilate into an English-speaking society (though they should be made aware that attaining a truly native-speaker accent is not achievable by most students and is not necessary in most contexts); alternatively, they may prefer to focus on achieving a high level of intelligibility in order to interact in English with a range of people around the world. This needs analysis may be determined by asking the students what they want to achieve, possibly by using a questionnaire, at the start of the course.

3.1 The Vocal Tract

Teaching or reviewing essential parts of the vocal tract with students at the beginning of a language course can help them access the descriptions of consonant and vowel sound production later in the course. While some phonetics publications, such as Laver (1994) and Ladefoged (2001), contain detailed descriptions of the speech organs, it is not necessary to introduce the vocal tract in minute detail to most language learners. Rather, instructors might just identify the anatomical parts that are essential to the production of the phonemes in the target language. This is most helpfully done by displaying a sagittal diagram, a cross-sectional view of the head, such as in Figure 1.

In addition to visual support, lower-level students may benefit from the use of simplified labels. For example, rather than teaching the technical term *alveolar ridge* to English learners, educators may prefer to use the more accessible term *tooth ridge*. An interactive activity in which students work together to label copies of a sagittal diagram can be a fun way to cover this key vocabulary in a classroom setting. Alternatively, teachers can provide students with cardboard, plastic tubes, and a pump and have them work in small groups to build models of the vocal tract.

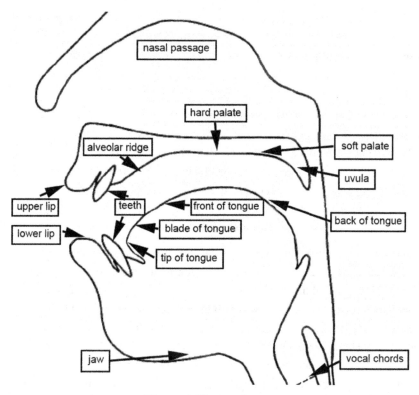

Figure 1 The vocal tract

For learners who have not previously given much thought to their vocal tracts, other tools can achieve awareness raising. Mirrors can help them identify both external and internal parts of the vocal tract, such as the lips, teeth, and parts of the tongue (Ladefoged, 2001, p. 100). Moving small lollipops around their mouths can familiarize students with anatomical features that are harder to see, such as the alveolar ridge, hard palate, and velum. In addition, feathers or small slips of paper can help them see the movement of air as it is exhaled through the mouth and nose. Since learning about phonemes is a physical as well as a mental process, techniques which utilize auditory, visual, and kinesthetic modalities can raise awareness about aspects of English pronunciation that might otherwise go unnoticed (Acton et al., 2013; Zielinski & Yates, 2014, p. 68).

It is also helpful to combine learning about articulation with phonetic transcription, as previously discussed in Section 2. For example, it can be useful to get students to identify the speech organs in their vocal tract starting from the lips at the front, produce sounds in different locations, and transcribe those sounds using the IPA. Teachers can put students in pairs, asking one partner to produce a sound and the other to identify the articulation process and write down the symbol for the sound.

3.2 Articulation: Consonants

Most consonants are formed by bringing parts of the vocal tract, known as *articulators*, in contact in order to obstruct the air flow, either partially or fully. The point at which the articulators touch or nearly touch is called the *place of articulation*. The places of articulation include the lips, teeth, tongue, alveolar ridge, hard palate, and velum (soft palate).

3.2.1 Place of Articulation

In order to accurately pronounce the consonant phonemes of the target language, students need to learn how to position their articulators appropriately. This may be challenging for them for three reasons. First, they may not perceive the sounds accurately. In other words, if the phoneme does not exist in their L1, learners may not hear it in the same way that a proficient L1 user hears it – something Hayes-Harb and Masuda (2008) refer to as *foreign-accented listening*. For instance, many Japanese-speaking learners hear /ɹ/ and /l/ as the same sound because they are not distinguished in Japanese, so they may be unable to differentiate between words such as *right* and *light* (Haslam, 2018, p. 2). Second, leaners may not be accustomed to positioning their articulators in certain ways. For example, learners of English whose first languages do not contain the /θ/ or /ð/ sounds may not be accustomed to positioning their tongues between their teeth, and they may need explicit instruction and repeated practice to master this placement. Third, while consonant sounds sometimes seem similar across languages, the place of articulation may differ slightly. If students are unaware of this difference, they may have problems accurately pronouncing the target phoneme. For example, the Spanish /t/ sound is dental in articulation, and native speakers touch the tip and front of the tongue on the back of the upper teeth (Salcedo, 2010). This position is different from the English /t/, in which only the tip of the tongue touches the alveolar ridge (Ladefoged, 2001).

In English, there are seven places of articulation for consonant sounds, and students may need to be familiar with other places of articulation (such as uvular; see Figure 1) to understand how the sounds of other languages are produced, and how their own articulation of English may differ from what is expected. It should be noted that, while learning the terms associated with the place of articulation may be helpful for teachers, language learners may not benefit from memorizing these terms. Instead, educators might want to present the sounds using simple explanations, visuals, and example words. Table 4 includes sagittal diagrams to illustrate the articulation of English consonants. Note that these sagittal diagrams are not completely accurate for the nasal sounds /m, n, ŋ/, in which the velum is lowered to allow air to pass out through the nose.

Table 4 Place of articulation for English consonants (based on Celce-Murcia et al., 2010, p. 61)

Place	Articulation	Sagittal Diagram	Examples
Bilabial	upper and lower lips together or (for /w/) almost together		/b/ – buy /p/ – pie /m/ – my /w/ – why
Dental	tongue touches upper front teeth or protrudes between the teeth		/θ/ – thank /ð/ – these
Labio-dental	lower lip touches upper teeth		/f/ – fan /v/ – van
Alveolar	tongue touches or nearly touches alveolar ridge		/t/ – tip /d/ – dip /s/ – sip /z/ – zip /l/ – lip /n/ – nip
Palatal (post-alveolar)	front and middle of tongue moves toward or touches the alveolar ridge and front of hard palate		/ʃ/ – sure /ʒ/ – measure /ʧ/ – chill /ʤ/ – Jill /j/ – yip /ɹ/ – rip
Velar	back of tongue touches the velum		/k/ – could /g/ – good /ŋ/ – king
Glottal	air passes unimpeded through the vocal tract		/h/ – hat

Sagittal images such as those included in Table 4 do not always illuminate the place of articulation as efficiently as one might hope because, as Gilbert

(1991, p. 312) reminds us, the crucial mouth relationships are actually three dimensional. A few techniques may facilitate the learning of articulation:

1. Instructors can provide a model of the place of articulation using their own face and encourage students to mimic it. A mirror can help students determine the configuration of the lips and the tip of the tongue (Ladefoged, 2001, p. 100). Alternatively, they may use online resources such as Sounds of Speech, mentioned earlier, which contains animated sagittal diagrams.
2. For consonant sounds that involve placement of the tongue, Miller (2011) recommends teachers use a red sock on their hand to highlight the correct position for the tongue. To perfect the mouth position for pronouncing the dental phonemes with an interdental articulation, students can hold a lollipop or their finger (Noll, 2007) in front of their mouth and stick their tongues out far enough to touch it.
3. Gilbert (1991) suggests bringing dental molds into the classroom to demonstrate alveolar sounds, though presumably this tool could also be used for phonemes produced further back in the mouth.
4. Other strategies for helping students identify different locations in their mouths can also be useful. For example, English learners with varying L1s who pronounce /d/ or /t/ in place of /θ/ and /ð/ can dip a cotton swab into lemon juice and rub it on their alveolar ridge (Noll, 2007). If they taste lemon as they are repeating words beginning with the dental phonemes, they are touching their tongue to the tooth ridge instead of pressing it up against the top teeth or inserting it between the teeth.

3.2.2 Manner of Articulation

In addition to being conscious about where consonant sounds occur in their mouths, language learners also need to know how air is released as the sounds are produced. This is known as the *manner of articulation*. Ladefoged (2001, p. 101) compares the production of sounds to water passing through a garden hose, in that you can do various things to the hose to influence the flow of the water.

Language learners may struggle to produce consonant sounds correctly because they are accustomed to restricting their airflow in different ways. For example, while Spanish has an /r/ sound, it tends to be trilled, with the tip of the tongue tapping rapidly on the alveolar ridge (Avery & Ehrlich, 1992c; Coe, 2001); in contrast, the English /ɹ/ is formed without touching the alveolar ridge at all, and while use of a Spanish trill is unlikely to cause problems in intelligibility, it results in a noticeable foreign accent (Rogerson-Revell, 2018, p. 97). However, in many cases, the substitution of a target-language phoneme with a more familiar L1 sound can be problematic for intelligibility. For instance, Korean does not contain /f/, a sound that involves a kind of hissing that we call a *fricative*, and rather than narrowing their airstream by connecting their top teeth and lower lips in the labio-dental position, Korean speakers may say /p/, closing both lips in the bilabial position (Lee, 2001) and producing a stop instead of a fricative. This is problematic because the contrast between /p/ and /f/ carries a high functional load in English.

For the consonants of English, there are three categories describing how restricted the speaker's airflow may be: *complete closure*, where there is a complete stoppage of their airflow; *partial closure*, where the air stream is narrowed by articulators nearly touching, resulting in a fricative; and *approximation*, where the air stream is narrowed by articulators coming close to one another but not as close as for a fricative (Rogerson-Revell, 2018). In addition, there are two subcategories of approximant: *liquids* and *glides*.

The consonant sounds phoneticians refer to as *stops* (or sometimes *plosives*), /p, b, t, d, k, g/, are formed when the airflow is stopped completely by contact between articulators, either with a bilabial articulation, an alveolar articulation, or a velar articulation, and the velum is raised so air cannot exit through the nasal passage. This stoppage of air is brief and how it is released depends on where it appears in a word. If the stop is at the beginning of a word (as with the /t/ in *tack*) or the beginning of a stressed syllable in the middle of a word (as with the /t/ in *attack*), the release involves a puff of air. The duration of this puff of air before the onset of voicing of the following segment is referred to as *voice onset time* (VOT). For /p, t, k/, the puff of air is audible and is often referred to as *aspiration*; however, for /b, d, g/, the puff of air is weaker and less noticeable. The contrast between the strength of the aspiration is occasionally referred to as *fortis* (strong) for /p, t, k/ and *lenis* (weak) for /b, d, g/. When these sounds appear at the beginning of an unstressed syllable (as with the /t/ in *attic*) or at the end of a syllable (as with the /t/ in *hat*), the plosion "is very weak and often not audible" (Roach, 2009, p. 28) regardless of whether they are *fortis* or *lenis*, and English listeners tend to distinguish between word-final *fortis* and *lenis* stops based on the length of the preceding vowel sound. The vowel before word-final /p, t, k/ is held for a shorter period of time than the same vowel sound before /b, d, g/. For instance, the /æ/ sound before /t/ in *pat* is shorter than the /æ/ sound in *pad*.

Fricatives are produced when the articulators are touching or nearly touching, but the passage of air through the mouth is not completely closed off. In English, there are nine fricatives: /f, v, θ, ð, s, z, ʃ, ʒ, h/. The restricted air passage in the vocal tract can have labio-dental articulation, dental articulation, alveolar articulation, palatal articulation, or glottal articulation, and a hissing sound occurs as a result of the turbulence in the airstream as it passes between the articulators in close contact. English learners may conflate stops for fricatives, as in *berry* instead of *very* or *copy* instead of *coffee*. When this happens, teachers can use pictures or themselves as models to draw learners' attention to the narrow opening associated with the target fricative and compare that with the closed mouth position of the stop consonant, while students use mirrors to see and correct their own articulation. Encouraging students to hold their hands in front of their mouths to compare the sustained stream of air of a fricative with the burst of air of a stop can also help clarify the difference between fricatives and stops.

In English, there are two sounds that are a combination of a stop and a fricative, /tʃ/ and /dʒ/, and they are known as *affricates*. When speakers make these sounds, their tongues touch the alveolar ridge, stopping the airflow. Then, instead of a sharp release to produce a stop, the contact between the articulators is slowly released, and there is a fricative following the stop (Ladefoged & Johnson, 2011, p. 15). Some English students, particularly Spanish and Portuguese speakers, have trouble contrasting the fricative /ʃ/ and the affricate /tʃ/ (Avery & Ehrlich, 1992c). Teachers might give Spanish-speaking students small plastic spoons to put upside down over their tongues (Noll, 2007). As they start to make the /tʃ/ sound, the spoon may block the tongue from touching the alveolar ridge, producing the /ʃ/ sound instead. Alternately, Portuguese-speaking learners might benefit from the lemon juice trick if they are substituting /ʃ/ for /tʃ/. If they taste the lemon juice, they have touched their tongue to their alveolar ridge, forming the target sound correctly.

Although most consonant sounds are formed by air passing through the oral cavity, three English sounds occur when air passes through the nasal cavity. These sounds, /m, n, ŋ/, are called *nasals*, and students are often amused to discover that it is impossible to produce these sounds when their noses are plugged. The places of articulation are different for each of these sounds (/m/ is bilabial, /n/ is alveolar and /ŋ/ is velar), but the air is stopped at each of the points of articulation in the same way that it is for a stop consonant. The difference is that the velum is lowered, and the air passes out through the nose, and some students may have difficulty producing a clear nasal in some circumstances. For example, speakers of English in Hong Kong may confuse /n/ and /l/ (Deterding et al., 2008), and Russian speakers may produce /ŋ/ as /g/, so *wing* sounds like *wig* (Monk & Burak, 2001). If students show difficulty producing a nasal sound, Gilbert (1991) suggests having them hold a mirror under their nose and say /n/ or /ŋ/. The mirror will fog up if they are correctly allowing air through their nasal passage but not if they are incorrectly saying /l/ or /g/.

Approximants are formed when the articulators come into close contact, but they do not actually touch. In other words, "the space between the articulators is wide enough to allow the airstream through with no audible friction" (Collins & Mees, 2009, p. 48). There are two types of approximants in English: the *liquids*, /l/ and /ɹ/ (the latter being the approximant at the start of *red*); and the *glides*, /w/ and /j/ (the latter being the sound at the start of *yet*).

The liquids are some of the most challenging sounds for many English learners. /l/ is an alveolar sound, in which the air escapes along the sides of the tongue (Roach, 2009, p. 48). For this reason, /l/ is sometimes called a *lateral consonant*. /ɹ/ is another challenge for learners because in NAE the tongue does not touch the alveolar ridge or roof of the mouth; most speakers produce a *retroflex* sound by curling the tip of their tongues behind the alveolar ridge and rounding the lips slightly. Another fairly common way of pronouncing /ɹ/ is referred to as *bunched* /r/ (Carley & Mees, 2021, p. 30), in which the center of the tongue rises up toward the back of the velum and the lips are slightly rounded. In addition to these ways of articulating /ɹ/, the pronunciation of the sound also differs from dialect to dialect. Furthermore, in most dialects of British English, /ɹ/ is not normally pronounced unless it comes before a vowel sound, so while most North Americans would say *farm* as /fɑɹm/ and *far* as /fɑɹ/, in SSBE, the standard accent spoken in Britain, speakers would say these words with no /ɹ/ after the vowel (Wells, 1982, p. 76). English instructors will want to teach the pronunciation that is most useful for their learners.

As stated, /ɹ/ is notoriously difficult for some students and many substitute /l/ for /ɹ/ because they touch their tongue to their alveolar ridge or roof of their mouths. In addition to using sagittal diagrams, in order to help students feel the difference between the two sounds, teachers can get them to place a pen horizontally in their mouths between their teeth, as shown in Figure 2. When students say /ɹ/, they should not touch the pencil in their mouths; instead, the tip should curl around the pencil.

Lemon juice on the alveolar ridge can also help students identify when they are touching it with their tongue inadvertently and mispronouncing the /ɹ/ sound. English learners typically need a great deal of practice with this challenging contrast, and they often greatly appreciate any tangible help they can get.

The glides /w/ and /j/ are phonetically like vowels, but phonologically they behave like consonants (Roach, 2009, p. 50): they are articulated in ways similar to vowels, so the position for /j/ is similar to /i/ and the position for /w/ is similar in /u/; but they are used like consonants because they can occur before a vowel at the start of a syllable in words such as *wet* and *yet*. When English learners have trouble with these sounds, it may involve place and/or manner of articulation. For instance, Arabic and Turkish students may

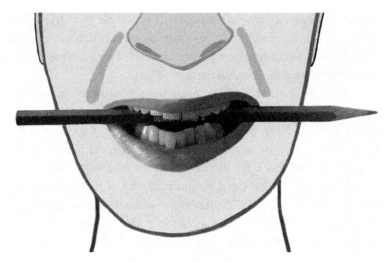

Figure 2 The pencil trick

pronounce /v/ (or possibly [ʋ], a labio-dental approximant) instead of /w/ (Nilsen & Pace Nilsen, 2010). Having students look into a mirror and compare their own mouth position with that of a model – either a picture, a video, or the instructor – is often enlightening.

3.2.3 Voicing

A final way to classify consonants is to distinguish between sounds that are created by vibrating the vocal chords, or *voiced*, and sounds that are created without the vocal chords, or *unvoiced*. More specifically, when a speaker makes a voiced sound, the vocal folds in the larynx come close together and vibrate, whereas when a speaker makes an unvoiced sound, the vocal folds are held apart. In English, the unvoiced consonant sounds are /p, t, k, f, θ, s, ʃ, ʧ h/. All others are voiced. All of the unvoiced sounds, with the exception of /h/, have an equivalent voiced pair in which the place and manner of articulation is identical; the only difference is whether the vocal chords vibrate or not. For instance, the mouth position for /f/ and /v/ are exactly the same; however, /f/ is not voiced and /v/ is voiced.

This voicing contrast can be challenging for some English-language learners because, according to Maddieson (2013), approximately one-third of the world's languages do not contain a similar distinction. Arabic speakers are accustomed to accepting quite a wide range of sounds as /b/, and, in learning English, they face the task of differentiating /b/ from /p/ (Field, 2014, p. 83). Because [p] and [b] are allophones of the same phoneme in Arabic, they do not distinguish words, and as a result, when speaking English, Arabic speakers may produce what sounds like /b/ instead of /p/ at the beginning of words, so *parking lot* may be pronounced as *barking lot* (Smith, 2001). In this case, teachers can have students hold fluffy feathers or small, thin strips of paper in front of their mouths while they are repeating minimal pairs such as *pit* and *bit*. The goal is for the feathers or paper to move more visibly when the initial sound is /p/ than it should for /b/. Alternatively, students can hold their hands in front of their mouths to feel the difference in aspiration with the contrast between the sounds.

Furthermore, when students' L1s contain voiced and unvoiced sounds, they may be constrained by rules most speakers are not even aware of. For example, speakers of some languages have trouble voicing consonants at the ends of words because voiced consonants do not occur at the ends of words in their native language. In addition, some languages have no voiced fricatives while others do not have voiced stops (Avery & Ehrlich, 1992a, p. 26). Some of these differences carry a substantial functional load. In other words, if a speaker pronounces *thank* as /ðæŋk/ instead of the expected /θæŋk/, most proficient listeners will be able to recognize this word without trouble because there are very few minimal pairs (for instance, *thigh* and *thy*) for /θ/ and /ð/. However, the possibility for misunderstanding is far greater for /p/ and /b/, /t/ and /d/, /k/ and /g/, /s/ and /z/, and /f/ and /v/ (Brown, 1988). To teach voicing, the difference can be demonstrated by placing the palm of the hand on the larynx when articulating contrasting sounds such as /s/ and /z/ and feeling the vibration in the latter. Alternatively, one can cover one's ears and feel the sensation of the resonance (Przedlacka, 2018, p. 40). In addition, since the unvoiced stops of English have more aspiration (the puff of air that is produced while saying them is greater) than the voiced stops, using a feather or a slip of paper may help students feel and visualize the difference between troublesome contrasts in syllable-initial position.

3.3 Articulation: Vowels

The classification of consonant sounds that was outlined in Section 3.2 does not apply to the description of vowels, as this requires information about tongue height, tongue position, lip rounding, and tenseness (either tense or lax). In some ways, this is more challenging than the description of consonants, because there is considerable space between the articulators, and the air flows relatively unobstructed between them (Rogerson-Revell, 2018, p. 108). As a result, students often have trouble understanding what the target mouth position is and what they are doing wrong when they cannot achieve the appropriate sound. In addition to being difficult to describe, model, and recreate, vowel sounds are challenging for learners because there are more vowel phonemes in English than in most other languages, which typically have five to eight vowels (Maddieson, 1984). Most speakers of NAE have twelve simple vowels (or monophthongs, involving a single target) and three diphthongs (involving two targets), and teachers can expect that many students will have difficulties mastering all the vowels of English (Celce-Murcia et al., 2010, p. 134). Furthermore, vowel sounds vary, both in quality and length, between English dialects. Finally, English vowel sound-spelling correspondence is notoriously loose. While it is true that the spelling conventions for consonant sounds can occasionally be mystifying, every single vowel sound in English has multiple potential spellings. Students whose L1 sound-spelling correspondence is more straightforward, for example as it is in Spanish (Coe, 2001), may find both the pronunciation and the spelling of English vowels challenging.

However, mastering English vowel sounds is important, particularly for students whose purpose in learning English is to communicate with native speakers, because of the role of vowel sounds in word stress. Grosjean and Gee (1987) describe the stressed syllable in a word as providing an access code to the listener. If the peak vowel of the stressed syllable is mispronounced, the access code may be difficult for the listener to process. Nevertheless, Jenkins (2007) suggests that some flexibility may be acceptable in the production of English vowel quality in ELF contexts.

When educators introduce the English vowel sounds, it can be helpful to draw attention to the four basic features: tongue height, or how close the tongue is to the roof of the mouth; tongue position, or which part of the tongue is highest; lip shape, either rounded or spread; and tense versus lax (Celce-Murcia et al., 2010; Collins & Mees, 2009, p. 59). Tongue height can be high, mid, or low, while tongue position can be front, central, or back, and, conventionally, the quality of the vowels in terms of these two dimensions can be represented on a vowel quadrant, as in Figure 3 which shows the quality of the simple vowels of NAE. (A two-dimensional plot like this cannot show details about roundedness or tenseness; these two features will be discussed in Sections 3.3.3 and 3.3.4.)

For SSBE, an additional vowel is /ɒ/, the vowel in words such as *hot*, which has a low-back quality similar to that shown for /ɔ/ in Figure 3, while /ɔ/ has a less open quality (Cruttenden, 2014, pp. 126 & 129). One vowel that is not shown in Figure 3 is the short midcentral vowel represented by the symbol /ə/ and known as the *schwa*. It only occurs in unstressed syllables and will be discussed further in Section 4.2 in connection with word stress.

Because students may struggle to differentiate between all these vowel sounds and some may find phonetic symbols intimidating, assigning each vowel sound

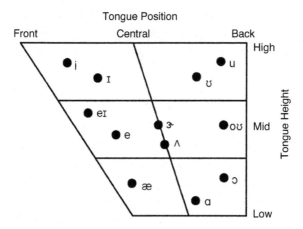

Figure 3 Vowel quadrant showing the quality of the twelve simple vowels of NAE in terms of tongue height and tongue position

a touchstone word can be useful for reference. The Color Vowel Chart (Taylor et al., 2016; Taylor & Thompson, 2015) does this with colors in a highly engaging and effective way. The colors for the twelve simple vowels of NAE are listed in Table 5, but elsewhere, consistent with the claim that use of phonetic symbols is important, we only use the appropriate symbol to refer to each vowel. An alternative approach might instead adopt the color words to refer to them.

Table 5 The colors suggested by Taylor and Thompson (2015) for the twelve simple vowels of NAE

	Front	**Central**	**Back**
High	/i/ – green		/u/ – blue
	/ɪ/ – silver		/ʊ/ – wood
Mid	/eɪ/ – gray	/ɝ/ – purple	/oʊ/ – rose
	/e/ – red	/ʌ/ – mustard	
Low	/æ/ – black	/ɑ/ – olive	/ɔ/ – auburn

We now discuss each aspect of the quality of vowels, and how they can be taught, in more depth.

3.3.1 Tongue Height

In order to pronounce different English vowels, speakers need to adjust the vertical position of their tongue by raising and lowering their jaw. Some vowel phonemes, such as /i/ and /u/, require a high jaw and, consequently, a tongue held quite high in the mouth above its resting position, which is already higher in the mouth than for many other languages (Honikman, 1964). In fact, when many speakers are forming these sounds, the sides of the tongue may actually touch the sides of the back teeth. In contrast, when saying vowels with a low quality sound such as /æ/ and /ɑ/, speakers' jaws and tongues drop as their mouths open.

Students whose first languages do not contain as many different vowel sounds as English may struggle to lower their jaws as much as is required in NAE for the low sounds, particularly /æ/ (Avery & Ehrlich, 1992b, p. 99). Additionally, some students may have difficulty making the incremental jaw drops that differentiate English vowels. For example, it is common for speakers of English in places such as Singapore to merge /e/ and /æ/, with the result that *lend* and *land* are not differentiated (Low & Brown, 2003, p. 70).

To enable students to appreciate tongue height, teachers can instruct them to place a hand under their chins and encourage them to chorally repeat words containing the *high*, *mid*, and *low* vowel sounds, such as *beat*, *bit*, *bait*, *bet*, and *bat*, or minimal pairs like *lit* and *let*, and *send* and *sand*. As the students repeat the words, their hands can track the movement of their jaws. Mirrors can also help them to see this movement if they repeat the words while comparing jaw movements of their instructor (or a video model) with their own reflection.

3.3.2 Tongue Position

In concert with the raising and lowering of the jaw (and along with it, the tongue), different parts of the tongue are raised and lowered in the pronunciation of different vowel sounds. For the front vowels /i, ɪ, eɪ, e, æ/, the front part of the tongue is raised. In contrast, when speakers articulate the back vowels, /u, ʊ, oʊ, ɔ/, the back part of the tongue is raised toward the velum. Finally, there are the central vowels /ɝ, ʌ, ɑ/, for which the tongue is in a neutral position, neither front nor back.

Because most people are not aware of the actions of their tongue during speech (Messum & Young, 2017, p. 37), it can be difficult to describe to language learners the tongue positions associated with the various English vowel sounds. Sagittal diagrams that show contrasting tongue positions, as shown in Figures 4 and 5, are useful for students to appreciate what their tongues should be doing.

Similarly, Messum and Young (2017) suggest using cuisenaire rods – short colored blocks of wood originally designed for use in the teaching of mathematics –

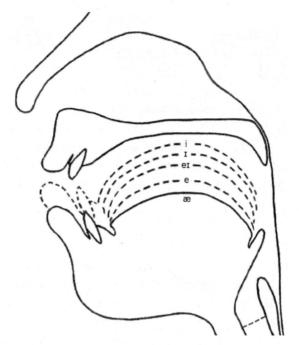

Figure 4 Tongue positions for front vowels

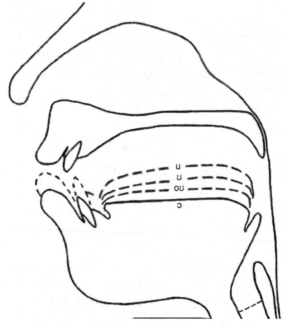

Figure 5 Tongue positions for back vowels

to build indicative bird's-eye-view models of the mouth so students can visualize the tongue movements in three dimensions. The authors recommend placing white rods in a semicircle to represent teeth and piling red rods inside the semicircle to depict various tongue positions. Miller's (2011) red sock also works in this way. Additionally, to give students a glimpse of the various tongue positions an instructor could rest a flat lollipop on his or her tongue and stand so as to be seen by the students in profile. When the teacher contrasts words containing front vowels, such as *beat* and *bat*, with words containing back vowels, such as *boot* and *bought*, the lollipop stick will move forward and backward. Ideally, students could each have their own flat lollipop so they can mirror the teacher's tongue movements.

3.3.3 Lip Shape

English vowels can be further distinguished by lip positioning: *rounded*, *spread*, or *neutral*. The rounded vowels of NAE are /u, ʊ, oʊ, ɔ/, and the vowels with spread lips are /æ, i, ɪ, eɪ, e/, while the remaining vowels can be said to have a neutral lip position. Typically, back vowels have rounded lips (Rogerson-Revell, 2018, p. 111), and since this is common to many languages, and also because it is easy to see, students may not struggle with this aspect of vowel production as much as they do with others. However, if students are challenged by the lip positions that these vowels require, they can repeat contrasting words after the teacher while monitoring their own mouth in the mirror.

Some languages, such as Mandarin Chinese and German, have a high front rounded vowel, represented with the phonetic symbol /y/ and often shown with the letter <ü>. Teachers of these languages may face challenges in getting their students to produce /y/; but teachers of English do not face this difficulty because this sound is not in the English vowel inventory.

3.3.4 Tense and Lax

A final way of categorizing English vowel sounds reflects differences in muscle tension in the mouth. The tense vowels are /i, eɪ, ɑ, ɔ, oʊ, ɝ, u/, and the lax vowels are /ɪ, e, æ, ʌ, ʊ/. Of these vowel sounds, the contrasting pairs /i/ and /ɪ/, as well as /u/ and /ʊ/, tend to cause English learners the most problems, and many students, such as those from Spain, produce the two vowels of each pair identically, using a sound that is neither the tense nor the lax vowel but between the two (Avery and Ehrlich, 1992b, p. 96). Students can feel the difference in the muscle movements associated with these sounds by placing their palms on their cheeks or by placing their fingers just above their larynx as they repeat contrasting minimal pairs after their teacher or a recording. It can be enlightening for them to feel their cheeks flex and relax as they repeat minimal pairs with, for instance, *heat* and *hit* for the /i/ and /ɪ/ distinction, and *fool* and *full* for /u/ and /ʊ/.

Tense vowels tend to be held for a longer duration than lax vowels. For this reason, tense vowels are often considered long, while lax vowels may be described as short. However, this distinction can be misleading as the actual duration of vowels depends on linguistic context, and a lax vowel might actually be longer than a tense vowel if it is the peak vowel in a focus word. Furthermore, vowels before an unvoiced final consonant tend to be shorter than before a voiced final consonant, which means that the vowel in *bid* may actually be longer than that in *beat* even though *bid* has a lax vowel and *beat* has a tense vowel. Figure 6 illustrates the duration of the vowels /ɪ/ and /i/ in the words *bid* and *beat* using a spectrogram generated in Praat (Boersma & Weenink, 2021). Although /ɪ/ is a lax vowel, in this case it is actually longer (0.24 seconds) than the tense vowel /i/ (0.17 seconds) because it occurs before /d/ while the /i/ occurs before /t/.

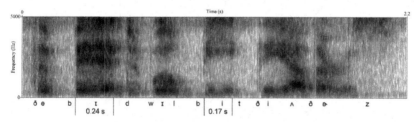

Figure 6 Spectrogram of a female speaker of NAE saying, "The bid will beat the others." Time is shown horizontally, and the frequency intensity of the various sounds is shown on the y-axis. While teachers and their students do not need to understand the intricacies of acoustic analysis, this figure does nicely illustrate the duration of the vowels in *bid* and *beat*.

Given that confusion between the tense/lax pairs can be problematic, it may be helpful to spend some classroom time on this contrast. Practice can be done via choral repetition with accompanying gestures, such as the thumb and pointer finger held close together for words with lax vowels and further apart for tense vowels.

3.3.5 Diphthongs

Diphthongs are also known as *complex vowels* because they consist of two vowel sounds starting in one vowel position and moving to another. Diphthongs can be regarded as tense vowels because of the muscle tension required to produce them. The three diphthongs of NAE are /aɪ, aʊ, ɔɪ/, and Taylor and Thompson (2015) assign the colors *white, brown,* and *turquoise* to these three vowels. In all three, the tongue moves from a low position to a high position, as in Figure 7. We should note that some people (e.g. Ladefoged & Johnson, 2011, p. 93) also regard /eɪ/ and /oʊ/ as diphthongs. However, the movement involved with these two vowels is rather less than for the three true diphthongs, so here we regard /eɪ/ and /oʊ/ as simple vowels (even though they are represented using two symbols).

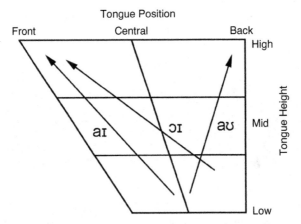

Figure 7 The three diphthongs of English

Students whose first languages have a more limited vowel system than English may not be accustomed to gliding between two vowel sounds to form a diphthong. Malay, for instance, has six pure vowels and three diphthongs (Clynes & Deterding, 2011), but the diphthongs cannot be followed by a consonant sound, so when consonant sounds appear after diphthongs in English words such as *like, loud,* and *coin,* the vowels may be realized as pure vowels with no appreciable glide (Yong, 2001, p. 280).

This pronunciation of diphthongs can be an issue because the use of a pure vowel instead of a diphthong is one of the most common pronunciation characteristics that results in a learner of English being judged as having a foreign accent (Roach, 2009, p. 20). To help students understand that diphthongs are essentially two vowel sounds, teachers may want to demonstrate the shift from one vowel to another by dragging their finger from the initial vowel to the final vowel on a vowel quadrant or vowel chart while slowly articulating the phoneme. In addition, mirrors can help students monitor their own jaw movement as they chorally repeat words containing the target diphthong.

3.4 Pedagogical Priorities

In selecting pedagogical priorities, four issues might be considered. First, it is valuable for language instructors to become familiar with how the consonants and vowels are pronounced in their students' native languages, specifically as they differ from the target language. Although it is often impossible for educators to become experts in their students' L1s, resources such as Avery and Ehrlich (1992c), Nilsen & Pace Nilsen (2010), and Swan and Smith (2001) can be helpful in identifying potential L1-related issues. However, Derwing and Munro (2015, p. 72) caution against relying uncritically on error prediction based on comparison between L1s and English, as there is considerable variability between learners – in terms of age, attitude, aptitude, motivation, and personal idiosyncrasies – even those with the same L1 at similar levels of proficiency. Caution is warranted in light of the lack of empirical support for tools such as CA, as proposed by Lado (1957) – discussed in Section 1.2. Therefore, instructors can attempt some sort of a needs analysis, perhaps by recording each student reading a level-appropriate text, to identify the actual phonetic challenges their learners face, and they should not rely too much on the deterministic predictions of CA.

Second, errors vary in the degree to which they cause problems in intelligibility (Derwing & Munro, 2015, p. 57). To help determine which phonetic errors are likely to have an impact on intelligibility, educators can look at the functional load of any two sounds, seeing how many words are differentiated by them; contrasts that differentiate few minimal pairs may not be important. Resources such as Brown (1988) provide details about how frequently certain minimal pairs actually occur in contrasting words in English, confirming for example that the /p/ and /b/ contrast is much more important than /d/ and /ð/.

Third, while this section has described the places and manner of articulation for the consonant and vowel sounds in NAE, local norms should be used to determine which variety of English to use as the target norm in the classroom. For example, in a midwestern or western US context and also in Canada, teachers may not want to highlight the difference between /ɑ/ and /ɔ/ because it does not exist for most speakers there. In fact, Carley and Mees (2021, p. 126) make a compelling argument for teaching only the phoneme /ɑ/ and not /ɔ/

because it is easier for students to learn thirteen vowel sounds rather than fourteen vowel sounds and because the use of /ɔ/ in NAE is declining in general.

Finally, classrooms made up of nonnative speakers who plan on using English mainly to communicate with other nonnative speakers in ELF settings may consider disregarding some features of native-speaker articulation. For example, Jenkins (2000) suggests that production of the dental fricatives /θ/ and /ð/ may not be necessary for maintaining international intelligibility, and the fine details of some vowel quality contrasts may also not be essential. Teachers should evaluate which sound contrasts in English are important for their students and adjust their teaching accordingly.

Once the determination has been made about which consonant and vowel sounds to cover within the constraints of a curriculum, instructors can begin to introduce the target phonemes with explicit instruction, relying substantially on visuals such as sagittal diagrams and modeling, as well as other pronunciation tools described in this section. In addition to guided production practice, listening discrimination activities are also useful pedagogical strategies, and focused listening by means of dictation is a valuable tool for enhancing skills in perception (Kissling, 2013). Certainly, the more practice that students get with producing and perceiving challenging target sounds, the better.

One crucial issue that should be addressed is how consonants and vowels are influenced by their context, and we now turn to this.

4 Coarticulation and Connected Speech Processes

The previous section surveyed the articulation of the consonants and vowels of English. However, these phonemes do not appear in isolation. They are parts of syllables, the unit of pronunciation that consists of a nucleus (typically a vowel) and surrounding consonants, and they occur in words. Where they appear in these words, as well as which sounds appear around them, has a substantial influence on how they sound in speech.

4.1 Consonants in Context

Unvoiced stop consonants are aspirated differently depending on where they occur in a word. When the unvoiced stops /p, t, k/ occur at the beginning of a stressed syllable, they are aspirated with some force. For example, in both *peer* and *appear*, the /p/ is produced with a burst of air, transcribed as [pʰ]. Students can easily detect this puff of air by putting their hand in front of their mouth when saying these words. However, if these unvoiced consonants occur at the beginning of an unstressed syllable (as in the /p/ in *super*) or after /s/ (as in the /p/ in *spell*), there is much less aspiration.

Figure 8 illustrates the lack of aspiration for /p/ when it follows /s/ using a spectrogram generated in Praat (Boersma & Weenink, 2021). In *pit*, there is a period of aspiration shown as [ʰ], the duration of which (the VOT) is about 0.10 seconds; but in *spit* there is almost no aspiration following the /p/. In fact, if one removes the /s/ at the start of a word such as *spell*, the word sounds like *bell* (Roach, 2009, p. 28), so removing the /s/ in *spit* would make it sound like *bit* to English listeners.

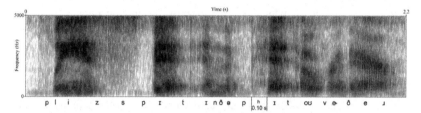

Figure 8 Spectrogram of a female speaker of NAE saying, "Please spit in the pit over there"

At the end of a word or syllable (as with the /p/ in *shop*), stop consonants are sometimes not released, so the closure for the stop continues and there is no puff of air whatsoever. The phenomenon of unreleased word-final stop consonants creates an allophonic variant of which English native speakers may be unaware. For example, the main phonetic difference between *can* and *can't* in fluent connected NAE speech is in the duration and quality of the vowel: the vowel in *can* (when it is followed by a main verb) is usually unstressed and produced as the short, midcentral vowel, the schwa /ə/, whereas in *can't*, the vowel is lengthened and produced as a full /æ/ vowel and whether the /t/ is aspirated as [tʰ] or else unreleased as [t ̚] is perceptually less important. Many people assume it is the presence of a final /t/ that differentiates these words, whereas in fact it is the quality and duration of the vowel that is key to the distinction. (Of course, in SSBE, this issue does not arise, as *can't* is usually pronounced with the back vowel /ɑ/.)

As discussed in Section 3.3.4, without aspiration to help listeners distinguish between the voiced and unvoiced stops at the end of words, they listen to the length of the preceding vowel sound. To help students perceive the contrast between the relatively long vowels that occur before final voiced consonants compared to the shorter vowels before unvoiced consonants, it may be helpful for teachers to present a list of minimal pairs, not just with stops as in *cap* and *cab*, *back* and *bag* but also with fricatives such as in *leaf* and *leave*, and *bus* and *buzz* (Grant, 2017); while students are chorally repeating after the teacher, they can hold their fingers close together for the shorter sounds and stretch them farther out for the longer sounds. Gestures such as these help to anchor the pronunciation within the student's memory (Morett, 2014).

Variation in the pronunciation of consonants can be problematic, and /t/ and its allophones can be particularly challenging, not just because /t/ may be unreleased at the end of a word, as discussed earlier. In NAE, when /t/ appears after a vowel sound or /ɹ/ and before an unstressed syllable, as in *water* or *parting*, it is often pronounced like a very fast /d/-like sound. This is known as a *flap* – the symbol for which is [ɾ] – because the tongue flaps against the alveolar ridge. In addition, speakers of NAE may pronounce a nasalized flap when /n/ occurs before /t/ before an unstressed syllable, so that the word *banter* sounds like *banner*. Some pronunciation experts refer to this as the *disappearing t*. In fact, in all varieties of English, /t/ can be omitted in a wide range of contexts, particularly when it occurs at the end of a syllable between two consonants (Cruttenden, 2014, p. 314), so it is quite common for there to be no audible /t/ in words such as *postman* as well as in phrases such as *best friend*.

While it might not be necessary for ESL students to master the flap sound or disappearing *t*, they do need to be aware of it. It is thus useful to provide a brief explanation, using visual support, of how the flap is produced, what it sounds like, and under what circumstances it occurs. Then, the instructor can have the students listen to words with and without the flap and have them identify which they are hearing by holding up one finger for the [t] sound, two fingers for the flap [ɾ] sound, and three fingers for the disappearing *t*.

Finally, in English, the /t/ at the end of words like *kit* and in the middle of words like *kitten* may be pronounced as a glottal stop ([ʔ]), with the airstream stopped in the throat as the vocal chords restrict. Again, while it is not necessary for students to be able to pronounce the glottal stop in order to be intelligible, it is often useful for them to learn about it so they can understand it when they hear it. As with the flap and disappearing *t*, a brief, level-appropriate explanation supported by visuals and followed by choral repetition may be sufficient.

Here, we have focused on /t/ to illustrate consonantal variation. In fact, all consonants exhibit variation according to context. For example, /n/ may actually be produced as [m] before a bilabial consonant in a phrase such as *green paper* or as [ŋ] before a velar sound in *ten girls* (Roach, 2009, p. 111). It is valuable for students to become aware of these changes when they are listening to colloquial, connected speech, though it may not be necessary for them to produce them in their own speech.

Field (2014, p. 87) recommends that, because there is no simple realization of each consonant, teachers provide practice at the syllable, word, and phrase level.

Students benefit from hearing and saying the sounds in the context of syllables, words, and phrases, so they can develop a large inventory of potential allophones for target sounds. For example, if students in the language classroom hear the phoneme /t/ pronounced as [t], [ɾ], [ʔ], and not at all (in the case of the disappearing *t*), they are less likely to be confused when they hear it in natural conversation elsewhere. Thus, when learning consonant sounds, studying them within the context of words and phrases is more effective than learning them in isolation.

4.2 Vowels in Context

Just as with consonants, vowels are influenced by the phonemes around them and by where they occur in words. Specifically, English vowels are shortened before unvoiced consonants, as described in Section 4.1; they are changed when they are followed by /ɹ/ and /l/ consonants; and, in native English-speaking contexts, they are reduced to schwa (/ə/) in many unstressed syllables.

A particular issue in NAE is how /ɹ/ influences the pronunciation of a preceding vowel within a syllable. These vowels can be termed *r-colored*. In SSBE, /ɹ/ only occurs before a vowel, so it can never occur at the end of a word or before a consonant. However, an <r> in the spelling has an influence on the vowel that is produced. Table 6 lists common uncolored and r-colored vowels in NAE, and the usual pronunciation associated with <r> after a vowel in SSBE is shown in the final column.

In NAE, when /ʌ/, and usually /ɪ/, /e/, and /ʊ/, are followed by /ɹ/, the sound transforms into the vowel sound /ɝ/. Some books (e.g. Celce-Murcia et al., 2010) do not list /ɝ/ as one of the phonemes of English, on the basis that it arises through context. However, others such as Taylor and Thompson (2015) advocate teaching /ɝ/ as a regular part of the NAE vowel system, and that is how it has been treated here.

In NAE, another noteworthy transformation undergone by r-colored vowels is the insertion of an [ə] sound before the /ɹ/. In some English pronunciation materials, such as Beisbier (1995) (and also in Table 6), the added [ə] sound is depicted as a small raised symbol, as in *fear* pronounced as /fiᵊr/, and it should be noted that this raised symbol indicates it does not constitute a separate syllable. In all these cases, in SSBE the vowel ends with /ə/.

A similar transformation occurs when /l/ follows the vowels, for example /i/ in *feel*, /ɪ/ in *pill*, /eɪ/ in *pail*, /e/ in *sell*, /oʊ/ in *hole*, /u/ in *rule*, /aɪ/ in *tile*, /aʊ/ in *howl*, and /ɔɪ/ in *boil*. This is known as *l-coloring*, and the same students who have difficult pronouncing r-colored sounds may also have trouble with l-colored sounds. Again, teaching students to insert a slight schwa before the /l/ can be helpful. Celce-Murcia et al. (2010) suggest demonstrating that words like *hire* / *higher* and *boil* / *loyal* sound similar, even though *higher* and *loyal* may be two-syllable words while *hire* and *boil* are usually one-syllable words.

Table 6 Comparison of uncolored vowels and r-colored vowels, with an example word for each in NAE and in SSBE

Uncolored Vowel	r-colored Vowel in NAE	r-influenced Vowel in SSBE
/ʌ/ – bus	/ɝ/ – burr	/ɜ/ – burr
/ɪ/ – stick	/ɝ/ – stir	/ɜ/ – stir
/e/ – pen	/ɝ/ – per	/ɜ/ – per
/ʊ/ – should	/ʊ°ɹ/ or /ɝ/ – sure	/ʊə/ – sure
/i/ – fee	/ɪ°ɹ/ – fear	/ɪə/ – fear
/eɪ/ – hay	/e°ɹ/ – hair	/eə/ – hair
/aɪ/ – fight	/aɪ°ɹ/ – fire	/aɪə/ – fire
/u/ – two	/u°ɹ/ – tour	/ʊə/ – tour
/aʊ/ – ouch	/aʊ°ɹ/ – our	/aʊə/ – our
/ɔɪ/ – boy	/ɔɪ°ɹ/ – Boyer	/ɔɪə/ – Boyer
/ɑ/ – hot (/ɒ/ in SSBE)	/ɑɹ/ – heart	/ɑ/ – heart
/æ/ – bad	/ɑɹ/ – bard or /e°ɹ/ – bared	/ɑ/ – bard or /eə/ – bared
/oʊ/ – foe	/ɔɹ/ – four	/ɔ/ – four
/ɔ/ – fought	/ɔɹ/ – fort	/ɔ/ – fort

In addition to being impacted by the sounds after them, the pronunciation of vowels also depends on where they occur in words, particularly whether the syllables are stressed or not, and reduced vowels are common in unstressed syllables. We discuss stress in English, how it affects the pronunciation of vowels, and whether it should be taught to learners of English in Section 5.

4.3 Connected Speech Processes

The changes which word forms undergo in spontaneous, casual speech are known as CSPs (Hieke, 1987, p. 41), and these CSPs have the effect of blurring word boundaries in continuous speech. As Goh (2000) notes, word recognition in connected speech is a major problem for second-language learners. Students accustomed to learning words in isolation may not realize that words in connected speech do not sound like their dictionary entries.

A variety of terms and classifications have been proposed for connected speech modifications (Alameen & Levis, 2015). Learner familiarity with these may aid speech segmentation and improve listening perception and comprehension. Unlike their citation forms, words in running speech may be contracted and/or linked, and sounds may be reduced, altered, or deleted to facilitate ease of articulation. Table 7 depicts the categorization of a select set of CSPs; the purpose of this set of CSPs is to illustrate some of the processes that occur in native speech, though the list is certainly not comprehensive.

Table 7 Selected CSPs with examples

CSPs	Types	Examples
Words Are Linked	consonants to consonants (same place of articulation)	*sit down, last time, some more*
	consonants to consonants (different place of articulation)	*last page, social media*
	consonants to vowels	*take on, talk about,*
	vowels to vowels	*key issue, go around*
Sounds Are Deleted	*h* deletion in sentence-medial position (for the words *he*, *him*, *her*, and adjective *his*)	*Is 'e busy? Did you meet 'im?*
Sounds Are Reduced	*can* becomes *kn*	*I kn do it*
	and becomes *n*	*Law 'n Order, wait 'n see*
	an becomes *n*	*miles 'n hour*
	of becomes *a*	*a lotta time*
	or becomes *r*	*right 'r wrong*
Sounds Are Altered	sandhi variation	*wanna, gonna, hafta*
	altered *you, your, you're*	*see ya, Is this yer book? Yer right!*
	d + you	*didja, couldja*
	t + you	*cantcha, dontcha, wontcha*
Words Are Contracted	negative	*isn't, aren't, doesn't, don't, won't, can't, shouldn't*
	auxiliaries	*I'm, I'll, I've, I'd, you're, you've, you'll, (s)he's, (s)he'll, it'll*
	modals	*could've, would've, should've*
	existential pronouns	*there's, there're*
	proper nouns	*Jane'll, Bob'll*
	common nouns	*the judge'll*

The question then arises: how many of these processes do learners of English need to master? A simple answer is that, while dealing with these processes is essential for comprehending spoken English by native speakers, none of them are essential for highly intelligible, proficient speech. For example, producing the word *and* as /n/ by omitting the vowel as well as the final /d/ may make learners more fluent but it does not make them more intelligible, and it is probably better in international settings to say /ənd/ or even /ænd/. Teachers therefore need to make students aware of the processes of simplification and deletion for comprehension, but learners do not need to master their use in their own speech to be highly intelligible in ELF settings.

4.4 Pedagogical Priorities

It is essential for learners of English to enhance their perception of the variable realization of sounds as they occur in context. Thomson (2018) suggests high variability pronunciation training as a means to do this, by presenting sounds in a wide range of different contexts. This will be discussed further in Section 6.

Familiarity with most CSPs is essential for the perception of conversational native speech, but many CSPs may be unnecessary for the production of highly intelligible speech, and some processes, such as those involving simplification and deletion, may even reduce the intelligibility of speech. Roach (2009, p. 117) argues that assimilation, the process in which one sound becomes more similar to its neighboring sounds, is sometimes given more emphasis in the classroom than is necessary; and Cruttenden (2014, p. 321) similarly argues that learners of English "need not attempt to reproduce in their speech all the special context forms of words." Dealing with CSPs is an area where teachers should make a clear distinction between the skills necessary for perception and those required for proficient production.

5 Prosody

We introduced the intelligibility principle in Section 1.1. Munro and Derwing (2015) elaborated the intelligibility framework and further categorized intelligibility into 1. local intelligibility – which refers to "how well listeners recognize relatively small units of speech, such as segments and words, outside of a larger meaningful context" (p. 381), and 2. global intelligibility – which entails "larger units of language that include rich contextual information" (p. 381). They suggested that instructors whose goal is to enhance students' communicative competence should focus on global intelligibility rather than local intelligibility. In this section, we focus on the larger units of language, which are often referred to as prosody, suprasegmental features, or the music of language (Wennerstrom, 2001).

Prosody is an umbrella term encompassing a number of pronunciation features including stress, intonation, and rhythm. Research shows that prosody may play important roles in intelligibility (Anderson-Hsieh et al., 1992; Derwing et al., 1998; Hahn, 2004; Levis & Levis, 2018). Challenges remain, however, in determining how these features should be described and how they might be taught. In this section, we first discuss the vital importance of prosody in language, as it is something that is learned early in L1 acquisition. Then, we focus on the teaching of prosody.

5.1 The Role of Prosody in L1 Acquisition

The importance of prosody for language learners is underscored by its central role in first-language acquisition by infants. Their perception of it develops early (Fernald, 1985; Quam & Swingley, 2012; Vihman, 2014), and Cooper and Aslin (1990) showed that infants are able to process and distinguish prosodic cues in adult speech shortly after birth. Mehler et al. (1988) conducted a series of experiments to investigate infants' ability to discriminate languages, their preference for specific languages, and the factors that influence their discrimination, and they found that infants as young as four days old are able to discriminate between their L1s and other languages, preferring to listen to their L1s. Subsequent experiments using filtered speech revealed that prosody is an important cue used in the discrimination process of infants.

Throughout infants' language acquisition process, the features of prosody (intonation contours, final lengthening, pause placement, etc.) play vital roles. For example, prosodic elements might support the learning of grammar and thus provide a child with a first step to "bootstrap" into the constituent structure of their language. Jusczyk and Derrah (1987) found that infants between seven months and one year old show a preference for pauses between clauses, even in filtered speech and nonnative languages; this finding suggests that prosody can help infants in locating syntactic constituents (or units). It seems, therefore, that prosody and syntax are intricately linked, and this link will be explored further when we consider the teaching of intonation later in this section.

5.2 Syllable Structure

Languages differ not only in the size of their segment (consonant and vowel) inventories but also with respect to the complexity and sequencing of segments in syllables. The syllable consists of a nucleus, usually a vowel sound, and optional elements preceding or following the nucleus. Any consonants preceding the nucleus constitute the onset, and any consonants following the nucleus are the coda. The syllable pattern of a language characterizes the number of consonants that may precede the nucleus in the onset and follow the nucleus in the coda. Languages with a simple syllable structure, such as Hawaiian, restrict syllables to just CV: a single consonant (C) in the onset, a vowel (V), and no coda (Davis, 2002). Languages with a slightly more complex syllable structure may permit additional consonants in the onset and one consonant in the coda, allowing CCV and CVC combinations.

English can have up to three consonants in the onset and as many as four consonant sounds in the coda. The phonetic structure of *strengths*, with this maximal CCCVCCCC structure, is shown in Figure 9, in which the syllable is shown with the symbol "σ." In this word, the /k/ appears phonetically, but it is not present in the underlying phonemic representation. The insertion of a segment not present underlyingly is a process called *epenthesis*; in this word, it allows a transition between two phonemes, the velar nasal /ŋ/ and the dental fricative /θ/. In a word such as *texts*, all four consonants in the coda /ksts/ are present in the underlying phonemic representation.

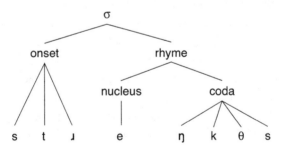

Figure 9 Syllable diagram of the word *strengths*

In two-consonant onsets in English, either the first consonant is /s/ or the second consonant is an approximant /ɹ, l, j, w/. In three-consonant onsets, the first must be /s/, the second must be an unvoiced plosive /p, t, k/, and the third must be an approximant. Other languages allow different combinations: so German allows /pf/ in the onset, as in *Pferd* (horse). Teachers of German need to get learners to master this /pf/ onset; but learners of English do not need to pronounce this combination.

The structure of English codas is complex. Typically, they can have a nasal or liquid followed by a plosive and finally a fricative such as /s/ or /z/ (representing the -s suffix) or /t/ or /d/ (the -ed suffix); but other combinations are possible, and learners of English need to be able to pronounce these complex codas.

Learners with L1s which prohibit alveolar fricative plus stop consonants in the onset often follow this restriction when they are speaking English. Thus, speakers of a language like Spanish may produce words like *Spain, school,* or *stop* with an initial unstressed vowel, rendering them as two syllables (Coe, 2001). Learners from languages with a predominantly CV syllable structure may avail themselves of two options with respect to word or syllable onsets or codas: either they insert vowel sounds to revert to their native language CV syllable structure, or they omit sounds. Both of these tendencies need to be addressed by teachers, as complex onsets are essential for the intelligibility of English.

Vowel insertion may also occur in word medial or final position. For example, all Japanese syllables end in either a vowel or the nasal /n/ (Scherling, 2012), resulting in a tendency to insert a vowel after every English syllable or word that ends with a consonant other than /n/.

Languages may also restrict consonants with respect to word position. For example, in the Thai language, the voiceless alveolar fricative /s/ is pronounced in word-initial position (Smyth, 2001), as in the greeting Swạ̄sdī – pronounced sà-wàt-dee /sɑwɑtdi/ – but not in medial or final position, as only four voiceless oral stops are permitted in syllable codas: /p/, /k/, /t/, and the glottal stop /ʔ/. Thus, failure to produce the unvoiced alveolar fricative in word-final position in English words – for example rendering the CVC word *rice* with a final glottal stop – occurs not because the speakers cannot produce /s/ but because they are not accustomed to articulating it at the end of a word.

One place to begin instruction is to take advantage of target sounds and sound combinations that do exist in the L1. For example, while Spanish prohibits consonant clusters with fricative /s/ plus voiceless stops in the word-initial position and would typically have an initial vowel, as in *escribir* (to write), it does allow this combination word internally, as in *transcriber* (to translate) (Coe, 2001). It may sometimes be possible to enable learners of English to produce complex clusters by making them aware that their own language has similar sequences of sounds even if not in the same position as in English, as appreciating this may facilitate their production in English.

5.3 Word Stress and Rhythm

Stress refers to the degree of force that is used in producing a syllable (Crystal, 2003, p. 435). Stressed syllables are more prominent than unstressed syllables because they are louder, longer, do not have a reduced vowel such as /ə/, and may be produced on a higher pitch (Roach, 2009, p. 73). Word stress is important for native English-speaking listeners as it provides them with an access code by which they store and retrieve words (Grosjean & Gee, 1987). Care should be taken not only to stress a syllable correctly but also to unstress it appropriately (McNerney & Mendelsohn, 1992, p. 187). If unstressed vowel sounds are not sufficiently reduced to create a perceptible contrast, listeners may not be able to pick out the stressed syllable with ease.

The vast majority of unstressed syllables are produced with the midcentral vowel schwa /ə/, which is articulated in a similar place and manner as the /ʌ/ vowel in words like *cut*. For example, in the word *photographer*, the stressed syllable, /tɑg/, has a long, clear vowel sound, but all the other syllables are reduced, so the word is pronounced as /fə'tɑgɹəfəɹ/ with a schwa in all syllables apart from the second one. Other vowels, particularly /ɪ/ (as in the second syllable of *traffic*), can also be regarded as a type of reduced vowel, but the schwa is by far the most common. Cruttenden (2014, p. 159) reports that nearly 27 percent of all vowels in English are /ə/.

Word stress, specifically using reduced vowels in unstressed syllables, presents a challenge for many English-language learners, as those whose first languages do not employ word stress, such as Korean (Lee, 2001) and Thai (Smyth, 2001), may have difficulty reducing syllables in English. Speakers of languages in which stress is fixed, such as French in which it is on the final syllable of a word or phrase (Hulst, 2014, p. 28), often also find English stress placement problematic. In addition, even when word stress is present in the L1, as it is in Spanish, learners may have a difficult time reducing unstressed vowels as much as speakers of English do (Mendelsohn Burns et al., 1992). Gilbert (2008) recommends having students pulling and relaxing a rubber band as they chorally repeat multisyllabic words so they can get the feeling of the contrast between stressed and unstressed syllables. Noll (2007) also suggests that students cross out the unstressed vowel sounds in keywords, so they are less likely to associate a full vowel with the written vowel in unstressed syllables.

However, in some English language classrooms, word stress may not be a pronunciation priority. Jenkins (2000, p. 150) regards word stress as "something of a grey area," so it is uncertain if it should be taught to learners of English or not, though in later publications (e.g. Jenkins, 2007, p. 24) it is excluded from the LFC – the inventory of sounds that is claimed to be essential for maintaining intelligibility – partly because it is regarded as "unteachable." Walker (2010) is also ambivalent about the importance of word stress. Although he claims (p. 39) that it has little impact on ELF intelligibility, he still suggests (p. 40) that it may be worth paying attention to as its role in ELF is not fully understood, and furthermore it has a role to play in sentence stress, which is regarded as important. (We deal with sentence stress in connection with contrast and emphasis in Section 5.5.)

While it has been argued by some scholars that word stress and vowel reduction are not crucial in some ELF settings, Lewis and Deterding (2018) have shown that unexpected stress can lead to a loss in intelligibility among speakers engaged in ELF interactions in Southeast Asia, so this is one reason teachers should continue to pay attention to it. Another reason to teach stress is that it is closely related to the rhythmic patterns of language.

Rhythm involves the repetition of something in time, but what gets repeated as the basis of rhythm varies. In stress-timed languages such as English, German, and Arabic, the stressed syllables tend to occur at regular intervals, while in syllable-timed languages such as Mandarin Chinese, French, and Spanish, a rhythmic beat occurs on every syllable (Abercrombie, 1967). While the rigid classification of languages into these two categories has been questioned (Dauer, 1983; Roach, 1982), measurements have confirmed that languages can be placed on a continuum of stress and syllable timing (Grabe & Low, 2002), though the best way of measuring the differences and thereby categorizing languages appropriately has still to be determined (Fuchs, 2016).

When English is spoken with stress-timed rhythm, unstressed syllables need to be spoken faster to maintain the beat. Roach (2009, p. 107) gives the following example sentence and says that, as the rhythmic beat falls on the stressed syllables (shown in upper case), the first syllable *walk* is extended while the three syllables *of the ca-* need to be spoken much faster.

WALK DOWN the PATH to the END of the caNAL

Teachers can demonstrate this regular beat by tapping loudly on the table when uttering each stressed syllable, and it is not difficult for learners to imitate this rhythmic production for simple utterances.

However, it is not clear if all proficient speakers of English around the world have stress-timed rhythm. It has been shown, for instance, that Singapore English has substantially more syllable-timed rhythm than British English, and there is much less syllable reduction in Singapore English (Low et al., 2000). The question then arises if teachers should insist on the use of stress-timed rhythm. Indeed, Jenkins (2007, p. 24) asserts that stress-timed rhythm does not need to be taught to learners in ELF contexts. We should note that the issue of stress-timed rhythm is closely related to word stress and also vowel reduction, and the extent to which these three features of pronunciation contribute to the intelligibility of English in ELF contexts remains uncertain.

We still recommend that all teachers should be familiar with the stress-timing /syllable-timing dichotomy as they will sometimes encounter discussion of it, and even teachers who do not insist on the adoption of stress timing may find it valuable to demonstrate it to students. Indeed, learners of English who decide they do not want to speak with stress-timed rhythm may note that familiarity with it can contribute to an appreciation of the meter of English poetry.

One feature of stress-timed rhythm is metricality, the tendency for an alternation between stressed (strong) and unstressed (weak) syllables to occur (Hogg & McCully, 1987). One possibility is to approach it via the metrical stress patterns of individual words, thereby linking rhythm with the acquisition of vocabulary. The teacher can therefore begin with alternating stress patterns of individual words before proceeding with the rhythm of phrases and longer utterances.

We start with disyllabic words since, as Cutler (1986) notes, stress alternates for most disyllabic and polysyllabic words. With the exception of compounds, such as *sunlight*, and polysyllabic words with full vowels in both syllables (e.g. *halo*, *window*, *typhoon*, *hotel*), disyllabic words fall into one of two possible stress patterns: trochaic (STRONG weak) or iambic (weak STRONG). Examples are provided in Table 8.

Table 8 Alternating stress patterns in disyllabic English words

Trochaic: STRONG weak	Iambic: weak STRONG
DIFfer	deFER
AWKward	ocCURRED
PERson	perCENT

As discussed at the beginning of this section, stressed syllables are longer in duration, higher in pitch, and louder than unstressed syllables, and stressed syllables do not have a reduced vowel such as /ə/ (Roach, 2009, p. 73). A significant challenge for English L2 learners is that lexical stress patterns for disyllabic and polysyllabic words are not easily predictable. To illustrate this, consider three three-syllable words for musical instruments: *piccolo*, *piano*, and *violin*. Even though all three come from Italian, in English they are stressed on the first, second, and third syllables respectively.

Having established the alternation of stress patterns in disyllabic words and the absence of straightforward rules for predicting word stress, the need arises for a pedagogical tool. One such tool is a lexical stress-notation system based on the findings of a study by Murphy and Kandil (2004), who conducted a stress-pattern analysis of the academic word list (Coxhead, 2000). Of the 525 headwords in the academic word list, thirty-nine stress patterns were identified, of which fourteen stress patterns could account for 90 percent of those words. Even so, teaching fourteen stress patterns is unwieldy. The authors devised a manageable numeric system for labeling stress patterns, which they considered useful when working with English for academic purposes and other ESL learners (Murphy & Kandil, 2004, p. 70). This is the notation system applied to the words for the three musical instruments mentioned above, with the first number indicating the number of syllables and the second indicating where the primary stress falls:

3-1   3-2   3-3
PICcolo   piANo   vioLIN

Once the notation system is introduced in class, two advantages emerge for vocabulary teaching. Students can be aided in learning how dictionaries indicate stress and encouraged to use a notation system for keywords in their English lexicon, and teachers can use or refine it for modeling a multisyllabic word's pronunciation when stress placement is at issue. The notation system can be simplified with increased classroom use. For example, "*economics*is a 4-3 word" can be reduced to "4-3" for instructional or corrective feedback purposes.

Having demonstrated the alternation of stressed and unstressed syllables in polysyllabic words, and tying this in with practicing new vocabulary, some of which involves learning quite long words with a clear alternating stress pattern, the teacher can proceed to the phrasal level, explaining that the same notation system can be applied to practice with preposition phrases, such as *at WORK* (2-2), *in the MORning* (4-3), and fixed phrases, such as *at FIRST* (2-2), *in the MEANtime* (4-3). To explain the rhythm of full utterances, teachers can emphasize that, just as with polysyllabic words and phrases, in English there tends to be an alternating pattern of stressed and unstressed syllables. Maintenance of this pattern depends crucially on the use of reduced forms, particularly for function words such as *of, and, for*, and *as*.

5.4 Intonation and Prominence

A narrow definition of intonation is the use of pitch on utterances. Figure 10 shows the pitch track for the utterance illustrated earlier in Figure 6 (Section 3.3.4) to illustrate the *bid/beat* contrast, showing that there is rising pitch on *bid* and also some rising pitch on *beat* followed by falling pitch at the end of the utterance, as is normal for a declarative statement.

A broader definition of intonation refers to the use of pitch as well as pause and prominence, also commonly referred to as sentence stress or focus

Phonetics

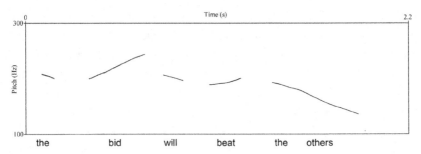

Figure 10 Pitch track of a female speaker of NAE saying, "The bid will beat the others"

(Pickering, 2018, pp. 2–3). Indeed, most treatments of intonation include prominence and other suprasegmental features as well as variations in pitch (Ladd, 2008; O'Connor & Arnold, 1973). Thus, we discuss the teaching of intonation and prominence together.

Scholars have approached intonation from a range of perspectives. For instance, focusing on discourse, Levis and Wichmann (2015, p. 139) refer to intonation as the use of pitch variations to communicate phrasing and discourse meaning (p. 139), while Bolinger (1989, p. 1) emphasizes the expression of affective or emotional information, stating that the primary role of intonation is to convey how we feel about what we say.

The different perspectives and approaches have led to confusion in teacher knowledge. To teach intonation effectively, language instructors need to adopt a learner-friendly approach, but this is complicated by the great range in descriptive techniques. Pike (1945) uses four levels to represent variations in pitch, O'Connor and Arnold (1973) suggest a range of complete tunes, Brazil (1997) introduces proclaiming (falling) and referring (rising) tones to introduce and refer to new information in his model of discourse intonation, Wells (2006) proposes distinctive pitch movements, tones, that are associated with tonic syllables, and Ladd (2008) describes a system of high and low tones aligned with accented syllables that was originally proposed by Pierrehumbert (1980). It is little wonder that learners are sometimes confused.

There is the further issue of whether intonation needs to be taught. While variation in the pitch of utterances is essential for successful communication, Jenkins (2007, p. 24) suggests that the exact pitch movements associated with native-speaker intonation do not need to be taught in ELF contexts. Nevertheless, this remains controversial, and many educators insist that intonation is vitally important, as explicit instruction on intonation can lead to substantial improvements in intelligibility (Derwing et al., 1998; Derwing &

Rossiter, 2003). Furthermore, even those students who choose not to closely imitate native-speaker patterns of intonation for their own speech will benefit from being aware of them to enable them to perceive some of the implications inherent in various patterns.

Pedagogically, teachers often encounter multiple challenges when teaching intonation. The first issue is learners' metalinguistic awareness. Students often do not have a clear idea of exactly why intonation is important for communication, and therefore seem to lack the motivation to master it (Paunović & Savić, 2008, p. 58). Reed and Michaud (2015) report a student saying, "If this [intonation] was so important, someone would have told us by now" (p. 461). Thus, we need to help learners to see the value and importance of intonation. Also, we need to acknowledge the limitations of textbook approaches, which often overemphasize its role in grammatical relations (indicating the end of a sentence, a question, etc.). In teaching, we also need to avoid overreliance on production-driven imitation (Gilbert, 2014) and establish connections between intonation and pragmatic functions and meanings. Levis (1999) notes that the characteristic textbook treatment is to emphasize the role of intonation in grammatical relations or conveying speakers' attitudes and emotions, and this may come at the expense of adequate attention to the pragmatic functions of intonation, such as emphasis, given versus new information, and implications. It is important for teachers to address these issues as well.

Here, we outline a metacognitive approach to the teaching of intonation that focuses on raising awareness about pitch movements, where they occur, and the implications they convey. The crucial issue is that students appreciate the importance of intonation in carrying meaning, especially when two sentences with the same words have different meanings arising from the intonation patterns adopted. For example, a simple utterance such as "It's raining" with falling intonation is an utterance, while the same sequence of words with rising intonation is more likely to be a question, or an utterance raising doubts about the weather. While we do not attempt to cover all the intonational patterns that can occur, as these are described extensively in sources such as Wells (2006), we provide an overview of efforts to raise awareness about the nature and role of intonation.

Key to the teaching of intonation is the raising of awareness, as recognizing its various roles is essential in getting students to accept the relevance of using a range of intonation patterns. Learner beliefs can be assessed using a brief survey at the start of the semester and again at semester end to determine any change. The following questions are from a survey adapted from Reed and Michaud (2015) to frame intonation instruction:

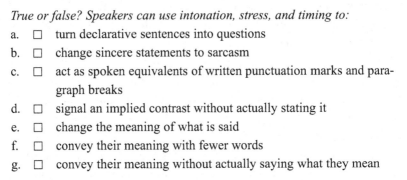

True or false? Speakers can use intonation, stress, and timing to:

a. ☐ turn declarative sentences into questions

b. ☐ change sincere statements to sarcasm

c. ☐ act as spoken equivalents of written punctuation marks and paragraph breaks

d. ☐ signal an implied contrast without actually stating it

e. ☐ change the meaning of what is said

f. ☐ convey their meaning with fewer words

g. ☐ convey their meaning without actually saying what they mean

Preinstruction survey results can be informative for both learner and instructor. Native-speaker instructors, in particular, who intuitively know that all these functions are possible, may find it eye opening if their learners reject a role for intonation in accomplishing these functions. As Gilbert (2014, p. 125) suggests, many students do not actually believe that intonation affects meaning, and it is important to overcome this view. Unless they can identify and understand varying intonational patterns, learners may understand the words but not the meaning (Vandergrift & Goh, 2012, p. 22). A metacognitive approach (Goh, 2008) requires students to detect, locate, and interpret the intonational signal for emphasis, contrasts, implications, and inferences. Here, some steps in a metacognitive approach to the teaching of intonation are outlined.

As a preliminary exercise, intonation instruction can be introduced at the level of monosyllabic words by presenting contrastive stress with accompanying intonation. Teachers can illustrate that lengthening the duration of the vowel in the stressed words allows for the superimposition of a pitch contour, as in the following two example sentences. (In this section, the words with special, contrastive focus are bold and in italics. They are not in upper case, as in the previous sections, because here we are discussing contrastive focus rather than word stress.)

Did you order a ***small*** one or a ***large*** one?

Don't turn the radio ***off***, turn it ***on***.

To highlight the contrast, teachers can exaggerate the pitch movement. Some students may reject such exaggerated pitch contours used for contrastive stress as "silly" (Gilbert, 2014, p. 125), but teachers can point out that the purpose of producing exaggerated contrastive stress in class is to facilitate noticing it outside of class, as a prerequisite to perceiving intonation contours that are used to convey speaker intent. After introducing the pitch movements on monosyllabic words, the teacher can then proceed to illustrate a range of intonational patterns.

In the first step of the metacognitive approach, using the sample sentence below, students are asked whether two utterances, one with and one without the implicational fall-rise pitch contour, sound the same or different. (In examples such as this involving words with more than one syllable, the whole word is bold and italicized, not just the stressed syllable: "proFESsor" would show word stress, while "*professor*" indicates contrastive focus.)

Directions: Listen to the following two sentences. Circle "Same" or "Different" to answer the question.

Sound file 1: The professor didn't grade your papers.

Sound file 2: The *professor* didn't grade your papers.

Question: Do the sentences sound the same or different? Same Different

Once student responses consistently indicate that they can detect the difference, the focus can proceed to identifying the nature of the difference in intonation between the two utterances, including where the difference occurs and what kind of pitch movement is involved. It is crucial to recognize that the location of the pitch change has substantial implications.

Directions: Listen to the following two sentences and be prepared to explain the difference.

Sound file 1: She's not a *teacher*.

Sound file 2: *She's* not a teacher.

Explain the difference.

Students need to notice that in the first sentence the word *teacher* has extra pitch movement whereas in the second sentence it is the word *She*. Once they can identify the locus of the contrast, they can proceed to interpret it. In the first sentence, the referent may not be a teacher, but rather some other occupation, while in the second sentence, it is not the referent who is a teacher, but rather someone else. Ability to detect marked intonation and to locate its source is preparatory to the ability to interpret its function.

One function of intonation is to highlight new information relative to given or old information. Students may be aware of the role of articles in making this distinction, such as using the indefinite article *a* for establishing new information (e.g. "I noticed a student talking to a professor") and the definite article *the* for referring back to given information (e.g. "The student was asking the professor about an assignment"). While the contrast between *a* and *the* is crucial in written language, students' attention can be drawn to the role of intonation to make the given versus new distinction in spoken English, as in the following exchange in which bold is used to highlight the new information:

A: I'm working on an ***assignment***.
B: ***What*** assignment?
A: My ***homework*** assignment.

While *assignment* receives emphasis when it is new at first mention, it becomes de-emphasized once it is established in the conversational exchange.

Another function of intonation is to provide correction. Students can be asked to infer, for example, what was likely said by one person to evoke a response which involved a correction by their conversational partner. For instance, a response, "No, class meets ***Thursday*** next week" was likely made in response to a leave-taking utterance such as, "See you in class next Tuesday" by a fellow classmate. To correct a mishearing, as in the example below, contrastive intonation guides the listener to the locus of the error, in this case to identify which digit was incorrect:

A: Did you say the zip code was zero two one one five?
B: No, it's zero two ***two*** one five.

Contrastive intonation can also be used to guide listeners to make an implication not explicitly stated. Consider the difference between the two statements below:

1. She said she finished the assignment.
2. She ***said*** she finished the assignment.

The first is a simple case of reported speech, while the second implies that the speaker does not believe the assignment has been finished. This implication is conveyed by a fall-rise pitch contour on the word *said*, converting a statement of fact to an implication: but I don't believe her.

Implicature is a phenomenon whereby a speaker suggests something without literally expressing it. To illustrate implicature further, consider a classroom exchange in which a student requests a deadline extension and receives an answer with a fall-rise tone on *can*:

Student: Can I turn in my assignment late?
Teacher: You ***can***.

This fall-rise pitch has been called the *implicational fall-rise contour* (Wells, 2006, p. 27). In this case, it implies that the student will be penalized if the assignment is turned in late, and this is the opposite meaning from what a fall tone would convey if the teacher was simply granting the request.

As Wichmann (2005, p. 229) reminds us, intonation sometimes mitigates or even undermines the words spoken. In order for learners to understand what is meant, they need to be informed that intonation conveys meaning – in this case converting affirmative words to a negative message – and to know the mechanism by which this occurs.

We can expand this assignment deadline example to illustrate the implication of emphasizing one word rather than the other:

Student: Can I turn in my assignment late?
Teacher: *You* can.

Emphasizing *you* rather than *can* involves a different implication: it indicates the teacher is granting the request only to the student who sought the deadline extension but no one else. In the classroom, the specific meaning signaled by this kind of focus can thus be explored. Students can refine their ability to detect and locate implicational intonation with exercises in which they listen to recordings and circle the appropriate implication from among a set of options. For example, students can be presented with two recordings:

Sound file 1:   She's not a ***teacher***, _____.
Sound file 2:   ***She's*** not a teacher, _____.

Students are directed to finish the sentence they hear by choosing the appropriate option:

a.   she's an engineer
b.   he's a teacher

Following the instruction phase, diagnostic surveys can be used as summative assessments to detect students' conceptual grasp of the pragmatic functions of intonation in English. Successful responses to the postinstruction surveys will assess students' awareness that, in English, intonation can convey a range of different meanings, and will reveal students' ability to articulate that the mechanism is a change in pitch on the focus word(s) a speaker wishes to highlight. For example, students can be presented once more with the following two sentences and then asked if the papers were graded:

1. The professor didn't grade your papers.
2. The ***professor*** didn't grade your papers.

Successful responses to the postinstruction skill assessment will indicate that the two sentences sound different, that the difference is a change in pitch on the word *professor*, and that the implication in the second sentence is that the papers were graded but it was not by the professor. Students who respond that the papers were not graded have misunderstood the sentence: actually, they were graded, but it was done by someone other than the professor.

5.5 Teaching Priorities

Some of the issues discussed in this section are essential for students to master. The first one is the complex onsets of English syllables. While some consonants can sometimes be omitted from codas, such as the /t/ in *postman*, no consonants should ever be omitted from syllable onsets, and /s/ is rarely omitted anywhere. The only consonants that can occur at the end of syllables in Mandarin Chinese are /n/ and /ŋ/ (Duanmu, 2007), and learners of English from China often have problems with English, either adding an extra vowel at the end of a word or omitting consonants (Deterding, 2006). Similarly, speakers of English from Vietnam have no problem articulating /s/ in a syllable onset, but they often omit it from the coda (Hansen, 2006). These issues need to be dealt with, and reference to syllable structure seems essential.

This section also explored the teaching of the phonetic realization and communicative functions of intonation, based on three areas: what pitch movement occurs, where it occurs, and what meanings are conveyed by the pitch contour. A focus on teaching the phonetics of intonation is recommended to improve the ability of learners to understand speaker intent, as even speakers who do not aspire to adopt all native-speaker intonational patterns need to appreciate some of the implications involved in the utterances of people who do use them.

6 Advances, Issues, and Technology

In the above sections, we presented some of the phonetics knowledge essential for language teaching, but it is important to acknowledge recent theoretical advances, remaining issues, and emerging technology in phonetics and language teaching.

6.1 Phonetics: Knowledge, Skill, or Both?

We discuss the importance of phonetic knowledge in Section 1. Here, we would like to revisit the role of phonetics in language teaching with the focus on the different roles that phonetics plays for teachers and students.

For teachers, phonetics is both *knowledge* and a *skill*. When conceptualizing the role of phonetics knowledge in teacher cognition, the technological pedagogical content knowledge (TPACK) framework (Koehler & Mishra, 2009) is very useful. TPACK categorizes teacher knowledge primarily into three categories: content knowledge, pedagogical knowledge, and technological knowledge. The overlaps of these three categories lead to another four types of knowledge: pedagogical content knowledge, technological content knowledge, technological pedagogical knowledge, and the combination of all three, TPACK. If we map this framework to phonetics in language teaching, we can find that teachers need both phonetics knowledge and language-teaching knowledge. Teachers also need technological knowledge to facilitate and enhance the teaching of both speaking and listening (see Figure 11). Phonetics is also a skill for teachers. For example, as discussed earlier, teachers need to demonstrate sounds to provide examples and to help learners in establishing connections between the acoustic properties of sounds and their phonetic transcriptions.

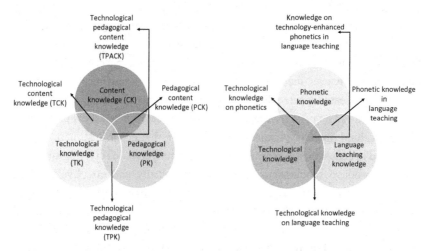

Figure 11 TPACK and phonetics in language teaching

While phonetic knowledge is crucial for instructors, it is less important for students to acquire that knowledge. Rather, language learners generally come to the class with the goal of using a target language to communicate effectively. For instance, as discussed in Section 2, while explicit knowledge of the IPA or another transcription system may promote language learning, having phonetic knowledge does not equal successful production of sound in spontaneous speech. Thus, learners do not necessarily need to memorize all the phonetic symbols and details of the articulation of all the sounds of English, and teachers may adapt the system to accommodate students' need. Phonetic knowledge can be used as a scaffolding technique. But it is important to acknowledge that the ultimate goal is to help students to be more intelligible, rather than having them memorize the terms we develop for this scaffolding tool. Educators should focus on how to transfer *knowledge* into *skills* involving controlled or spontaneous production of speech.

6.2 Research Informed Guidelines for Language Teaching

The past few decades have witnessed significant breakthroughs and advances in the fields of phonetics and language teaching. In addition, acoustic models such as the parallel encoding and target approximation model (PENTA model) (Xu, 2004) and the Fujisaki model (Mixdorff, 2000) have led to advances in technology in areas such as automated speech recognition (ASR) and text-to-speech.

In the field of language teaching, theories like complexity theory (Larsen-Freeman, 2017) and dynamic systems theory acknowledge the complex and dynamic nature of language development (De Bot et al., 2007). These theories point out that, to promote spontaneous production, teaching approaches and methods need to address the complexity of language at multiple levels as well as the dynamic relationship between language, the cognitive system, and sociocultural factors. However, there remains a huge gap between research and practice.

Phonetic research is often divorced from teaching because the two fields have different goals. The primary focus of phonetic research is to reveal underlying patterns behind phonetic features or phenomena. Language instructors, however, need to center their teaching around a different task – cultivating students' skills to produce spontaneous language dynamically and effectively. Thus, direct application of theoretical concepts or activities often does not lead to ideal results. As an example of an attempt to utilize a model of pronunciation in the classroom, Chapman (2007) tried to apply Brazil's discourse intonation model to teaching but found that even identifying rising and falling tones posed significant challenges for teachers and students. The teaching of pronunciation has generally been determined by ideology and intuition rather than research (Levis, 2005).

Language-learning research also often lacks a direct impact in the language classroom. There are many reasons why this is the case. One is that there is no unified theory identifying the schemata underlying the language-learning process, including, but not limited to, how explicit knowledge affects spontaneous production. Another issue is the substantial variability among leaners. The same method, when applied to learners with different L1s, goals, and learning settings, may yield very different results. Numerous variables including learners' attention and awareness (Schmidt, 2012), age (Birdsong, 1999), motivation (Waninge et al., 2014), and language aptitude (Wen et al., 2016) can all influence learning outcomes. It is unrealistic to expect language teachers to accommodate all these influential factors in teaching practice.

While direct implementation of research findings is often not an option, teachers can use the output of research to inform their practice. To this end, we propose the following guidelines:

1. The goal of language teaching should follow the intelligibility principle.
2. Students learning in different contexts (ESL/EFL/ELF) have different needs and objectives, and instruction should be responsive to these needs and goals.
3. Language perception and production influence each other and should both be addressed in language teaching.
4. Students' L1s affect perception and production of sounds in L2. Due to learners' perceptual differences, it is often possible to refer to a difference in articulation when helping them to produce an unfamiliar sound.
5. A consideration of functional load is useful in helping us to determine which sounds should be prioritized for instructional purposes.
6. To teach listening and speaking effectively, a transcription system is needed. The system benefits students the most if it is used consistently within and across classes.
7. Both segmental features (consonants and vowels) and suprasegmental features (intonation, stress, rhythm) are important. These features can be taught in isolation at first but need to be integrated in a dynamic system to stimulate spontaneous production.

Further, integrating phonetics with learners' communicative competence is crucial. Learners will benefit from authentic input and opportunities to use language in daily communication. Assessment focusing on their production of phonetic and phonological features in communicative contexts is more effective than assessing individual sounds or features in isolation.

6.3 Language Teaching with an Agile/Scrum Model

As we discussed earlier, despite efforts in connecting research with practice, there remains a huge gap between the two. One major challenge of language teaching is that there is no one-size-fits-all solution. For instance, educators who have students of the same language background may adopt a different approach than those who have students with different L1s. In language teaching, teachers often find that what works for one student may not work for another. Therefore, they need to individualize their instruction based on students' difficulties and needs.

Further, phonetic elements in language teaching need to be addressed dynamically with consideration of the complexity of the underlying system.

For example, when teaching consonants and vowels, teachers need to consider allophones and coarticulation. When teaching intonation, teachers will need to address both structural complexity (intonation encompasses a variety of inter-related phonetic features) and functional complexity (the use of intonation is influenced by many variables including intended meaning, pragmatic functions, and information structure [Liu & Reed, 2021]).

An iterative model, which allows teachers to adapt instruction within itera-tive, short cycles, may help them to manage the diversity of learners and the complexity of features. In software development, there has been a shift from a traditional waterfall model, in which project activities are broken down into sequential phases and compiled at the end of the project (see Figure 12), to what is called the agile or scrum model (Schwaber & Beedle, 2002). The scrum model, for example, is characterized by numerous iterative cycles called *sprints*, which typically last for one to four weeks. The idea is to develop software that has the basic functions and then improve it through rapid iteration (see Figure 13).

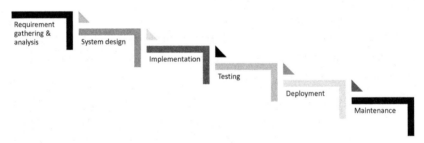

Figure 12 Waterfall model

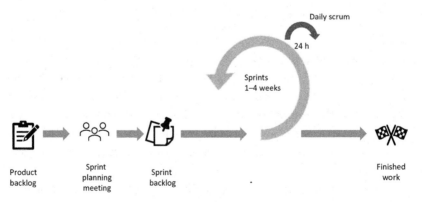

Figure 13 Scrum model

If we compare software development to language teaching, we may find some similarities. For example, both software and language are for pragmatic use, both include multiple features, and both are used dynamically. To apply the agile model in language teaching, teachers need to view language as a whole system consisting of multiple subsystems that need to be improved. The difference between the traditional model and the agile model of language teaching is visualized in Table 9.

Table 9 Traditional vs. agile approach to language teaching

Traditional Approach	Agile/Scrum Approach
• Phonetic and phonological features are taught mostly in isolation. The system emerges at the end of the teaching period.	• Phonetic and phonological features are taught as a whole system with multiple subsystems. This system, though not mature, exists at the beginning of the teaching period.
• Progress is characterized by adding new knowledge and skills about individual features: $N + 1, N + 2 \ldots$	• Progress is characterized by continuous development of the whole system: $N\ 1.0, N\ 2.0, N\ 3.0 \ldots$
• Assessment focuses on individual features after small learning cycles.	• Assessment is also conducted at the whole system level, although feedback is provided for the subsystems.

Note that in an agile/scrum approach, teachers can still focus on an individual feature each week or every teaching cycle. But improvement is only considered to have occurred when the individual feature is successfully integrated to the whole system.

It may be helpful to use a metaphor to clarify this. Traditionally, if we want to build a car, we design and manufacture individual components such as the engine, wheels, and transmission first. We intend to make all parts with the highest quality possible, and then we assemble them. The agile/scrum model is different: assuming we already have a car that can run (but maybe only at a speed of twenty miles per hour), our goal is to improve this car. In the first week, we may take out the engine, redesign it, and then put it back in. In the second week, we take the transmission out, improve it, and then put it back in. The car is in constant improvement and is always evaluated as a whole. Further, instead of measuring the performance of different parts, we use how fast and smooth the car can run as the indicator of improvement.

Second-language development is a similar process. A student has an interlanguage system (Selinker, 1972). If we break the system into different parts and focus on one aspect at a time, students may be able to use the feature in isolation, but they may not be able to "assemble" it within the interlanguage system. For example, a student may be able to produce the intonation of a model sentence perfectly but does not or cannot use it together with other features in daily communication. Thus, instead of breaking the language system into different components, teachers may view it as a whole system and aim for improvement at the interlanguage level. To achieve this, teachers can still focus on individual skills, one at a time in different lessons. But application and assessment need to be done at the interlanguage level. For example, teachers can plan a "sprint" with the focus on individual sounds. Within the sprint, multiple minilessons can be implemented, focusing on the sounds that may hamper learners' intelligibility. Assessment of learners' interlanguage will be conducted at the end of each sprint. The next sprint can focus on prosody, which can be further divided into minilessons about syllable structure and about word stress and rhythm. Figure 14 visualizes this process.

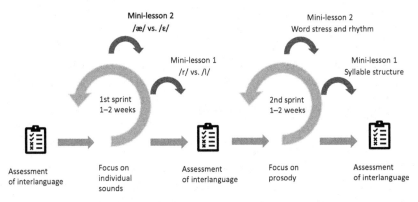

Figure 14 Agile/Scrum in pronunciation teaching

People often say that education is "flying a plane while building it." The agile/scrum approach puts this saying into practice. If a plane is not flying properly, we identify the parts (e.g. wings and tail) that could be causing the problem, fix them, and test them locally to make sure that they can function properly as subsystems. Then, we reassemble the plane and fly it.

It is important to acknowledge that improvement in pronunciation requires time, effort, and patience. Teachers may find that a student needs more time to develop a skill. They may also detect a setback in students' language production. The agile model allows teachers to gain feedback in a relatively short period and adjust their instruction based on the current developmental stage of the learners. The agile model also provides students with continuous momentum in improving their language skills.

6.4 Technology

Pronunciation teaching may be closely bound to technology, allowing teachers to perform a wide range of tasks from recording to evaluating speech (Cucchiarini et al., 2000). Some of the most influential technology includes speech visualization (Levis & Pickering, 2004), ASR (McCrocklin & Edalatishams, 2020), and speech synthesis (Ding et al., 2019). Despite significant progress in computer-assisted pronunciation teaching, issues remain. For instance, O'Brien et al. (2018) reported that "although technology is used extensively in pronunciation research, and is a growing component of language classrooms, some researchers and teachers express discomfort with new technological innovations: some implementations are difficult to use, and others are seen as unwelcome replacements for instructors" (p. 183). However, with rapid development in natural language processing (Lu, 2018) and artificial intelligence (Kessler, 2018; Li, 2017), we expect powerful tools that can significantly facilitate pronunciation learning and teaching in the near future. As technology matures, teachers can take advantage of existing technological tools to provide authentic input, assess students' progress, and promote intelligible output. To conclude this Element, we provide a short list of some existing technological resources for pronunciation instruction, along with the theoretical basis upon which we recommend these resources.

1. English Accent Coach (www.englishaccentcoach.com/)

   English Accent Coach provides assessment and perception practice of segmental features. Users listen to sounds or sound combinations and click on the IPA symbols that correctly represent the sounds that they hear.

Highlights: This website offers high variability input (Thomson, 2018) at the segmental level. High variability input can help learners to avoid focusing on idiosyncratic traits of a particular speaker.

Caveat: The tool is based on the IPA. To use it effectively, teachers and students need to be familiar with IPA symbols.

2. YouGlish (https://youglish.com/)

   YouGlish is a database with searchable YouTube videos. Users type in a keyword or phrase. YouGlish provides videos containing the keyword with a transcript.

Highlights: YouGlish offers authentic input at the discourse level. It also offers authentic materials for teaching.

Caveat: Because the materials are authentic, this tool may need to be adapted when used with language learners at lower proficiency levels; teachers may use the "playback speed" function to adjust the speed of the videos. They may also use the translation tools built into the website.

3. Google Voice Typing

Google Voice Typing is probably the easiest way a learner can get access to an application with ASR. It transcribes learners' speech into texts. Users can get access to Google Voice Typing by opening a Google Doc, selecting "Tools," and then selecting "Voice typing."

Highlights: ASR tools like Google Voice Typing may help teachers in determining learners' intelligibility to a certain degree. Research has found that learners can improve their language skills based on the feedback provided by Google Voice Typing, particularly at the segmental level (McCrocklin, 2019).

Caveats: The tool is not designed for language learning. Thus, feedback is highly limited and may not provide enough information to teachers and students, especially at the suprasegmental level. Although the transcription accuracy is at a high level for native speakers, learners' accents may lead to a lower transcription accuracy. When words or phrases are mis-transcribed, they could be either transcription errors made by the system or pronunciation problems made by the learners.

4. Sounds of Speech (https://soundsofspeech.uiowa.edu/)

Sounds of Speech provides animated pictures illustrating the articulation process of individual sounds.

Highlights: This resource allows learners to view a dynamic articulatory process.

Caveats: Knowledge of the IPA is needed for the identification of sounds. The sounds are also listed in isolation, so contextualized practice is needed to support students' learning.

5. Praat (https://www.fon.hum.uva.nl/praat/)

Praat (Boersma & Weenink, 2021) is software that supports recording, speech analysis, and speech visualization.

Highlights: This tool allows teachers to visualize both segmental aspects of speech and suprasegmental aspects of speech such as intonation and intensity. Such visualization has been found to be effective by researchers (Levis & Pickering, 2004).

Caveats: The software is designed for research and not for teaching purposes. While teachers can design teaching activities based on Praat, it may take a lot of time and effort to learn the software. In Sections 3 and 4 of this Element (Figures 6 and 8), we used spectrograms derived from Praat to illustrate variation in duration. The pitch contour in Figure 10 (Section 5.4) was also derived from Praat, but it was substantially smoothed. The raw-pitch track obtained in Praat is usually substantially less smooth, and it may include sudden jumps up and down. Learners of English often find English pitch tracks such as that hard to interpret.

7 Conclusion

Language use is a dynamic process involving multiple factors. To articulate an idea, a speaker needs to consider the grammatical and syntactic structure of the sentence, vocabulary, and pragmatics. Learners also need to produce consonants, vowels, stress, and intonation to produce speech that is easily intelligible. The process is similar to a juggler performing a circus trick, as illustrated in Figure 15.

The goal of this Element is to provide knowledge about phonetics to help language teachers to juggle the various skills necessary and also to evaluate what needs to be taught and what might be excluded. In addition, we hope that some of the teaching tips we have offered might encourage greater adoption of pronunciation teaching in the language classroom and provide helpful guidance about how it might be achieved. Finally, we hope that the sources we have referred to and the resources we have mentioned might tempt language teachers to explore more, to develop their knowledge about and skills in phonetics and thereby enhance the teaching of listening, speaking, and pronunciation in the classroom.

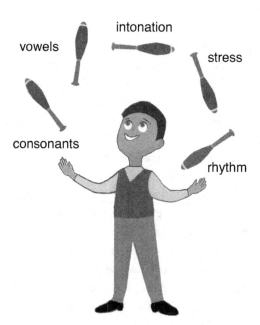

Figure 15 Juggler performing a circus trick

Glossary

affricate: A stop followed by a fricative at the same place of articulation. The affricates of English are /ʧ/ (the initial and final sounds in the word *church)* and /ʤ/ (the initial and final sounds in the word *judge).*

allophone: A variant of a phoneme that does not contrast with other sounds. For example, dark /l/ occurs at the end of a word such as *pill* while clear /l/ occurs at the start of a word such as *lip*, and dark /l/ and clear /l/ do not contrast, as their occurrence can be predicted from their position in a word. Dark /l/ and clear /l/ are allophones of the phoneme /l/, and they can be shown in square brackets: [ł] and [l].

alveolar: A sound produced by the front or tip of the tongue against the alveolar ridge, the ridge behind the upper teeth.

approximant: A class of sounds in which the articulators are close but not close enough to result in the hissing associated with fricatives. The approximants of English are /j, w, r, l/ (Crystal, 2003, p. 30).

aspiration: The burst or puff of air that is produced when plosives, such as the unvoiced English stop consonants, are released.

bilabial: A sound produced with the two lips closed or nearly closed. The bilabial consonants of English are /p, b, m, w/.

coda: Part of the syllable consisting of any consonants following the nucleus.

dental: A consonant produced with the tip of the tongue against the upper teeth or protruding between the teeth. The dental consonants of English are /θ, ð/.

English as a lingua franca (ELF): "Any use of English among speakers of different first languages for whom English is the communicative language of choice, and often the only option" (Seidlhofer, 2011, p. 7).

fricative: A consonant in which the air passes through a narrow gap in the vocal tract and sounds like a hissing sound; /s/ and /f/ are examples of fricatives in English.

functional load: The number of minimal pairs that exist for a given contrast. For example, the functional load of /f/ and /v/ is quite high, because many word pairs exist that only differ in their use of one or other of these sounds.

glottal: A sound produced at the glottis with no further restriction of the vocal tract. In English, /h/ is a glottal fricative.

iambic: Rhythm associated with a weak-strong stress pattern.

International Phonetic Alphabet (IPA): A set of symbols used for transcribing the sounds of language, originally developed by the International Phonetic Association in 1889 (Crystal, 2003, p. 240).

intonation: The system of variations in pitch in speech. Some definitions of intonation also include the use of prominence and pausing.

L1: First language.

L2: Second or nth language; target language.

labio-dental: A sound produced by the lower lip touching the upper teeth. The labio-dental consonants of English are /f, v/.

lax: A term used to describe vowels that are produced with less muscular tension than tense vowels. The lax vowels of English are /ɪ, e, æ, ʌ, ʊ/. Some people describe lax vowels as short.

liquid: A class of sounds that includes the alveolar approximants. In English, the liquids are /l/ and /ɹ/.

lingua franca core (LFC): The inventory of sounds that Jenkins (2007, p. 22) claims is essential for maintaining international intelligibility in English.

manner of articulation: How the sounds are produced. For example, if a passage through the mouth is closed completely, one gets a stop; but if air can pass through a narrow gap, a fricative is produced.

metricality: The tendency for stressed and unstressed syllables to alternate in stress-timed languages.

minimal pair: Two words that differ in just one sound. For example, *fan* and *van* are a minimal pair as they differ only in whether they have /f/ or /v/ at the start.

nasal: A sound produced with air through the mouth blocked off but able to pass through the nose because the velum is lowered.

nucleus: The central part of a syllable, usually consisting of a vowel or a syllabic consonant, such as [n̩] as in the word *kitten* [kɪʔn̩].

onset: Part of the syllable, consisting of any consonants that precede the nucleus.

palatal: A sound produced by the middle of the tongue and the hard palate.

phoneme: A minimal unit in the sound system of a language (Crystal, 2003, p. 347). Phonemes are shown in phonemic slashes, for example /t/ and /æ/.

phonetics: The study of the production, perception, description, and classification of spoken language.

place of articulation: The place in the vocal tract where the articulation of a sound occurs.

rhythm: The repetition of some unit of speech in time.

sagittal diagram: A cross-sectional view of the vocal apparatus seen from the side, with the head sectioned from front to back along its midline (Laver, 1994, p. 120). It is usual in sagittal diagrams of the vocal apparatus for the lips to be on the left and the throat on the right.

schwa: The short midcentral vowel /ə/ that occurs in unstressed syllables.

segmentals: Segment-sized sounds; consonants and vowels.

standard southern British English (SSBE): The standard pronunciation of English spoken in southern England; formerly the term "received pronunciation" was used. Roach (2009) prefers the term "BBC English," while Cruttenden (2014) opts for "General British."

stop: A sound made with the passage through the vocal tract completely blocked by the tongue or lips. The stops of English are /p, b, t, d, k, g/. Stops are also sometimes known as plosives.

stress: The degree of force used in producing a syllable. Stressed syllables are perceptually more prominent than unstressed syllables.

stress-timed rhythm: Rhythm in which the rhythmic beat occurs on stressed syllables and there tends to be equal timing between successive stressed syllables.

suprasegmentals: Sounds that extend beyond individual consonants and vowels, including stress, rhythm, and intonation.

syllable: A unit of pronunciation that is larger than a single sound but smaller than a word (Crystal, 2003, p. 447). A syllable usually has a vowel as its nucleus and may have a number of consonants preceding and following the nucleus. Words can be a single syllable or many syllables.

syllable-timed rhythm: Rhythm in which every syllable has a rhythmic beat, and syllables tend to have equal duration.

tense: A term used to describe a class of vowels produced with more muscular tension than lax vowels. The tense simple vowels of NAE are /i, eɪ, ɑ, ɔ, oʊ, ɚ, u/. The English diphthongs are also tense. Tense vowels are described by some people as long.

trochaic: Rhythm associated with a strong-weak stress pattern.

velar: A sound made with the back of the tongue against the velum (also known as the soft palate). The velars of English are /k, g, ŋ/.

vocal tract: The air passage above the glottis used in producing speech.

voice onset time (VOT): The delay in the start of voicing after the release of a stop; VOT indicates the duration of aspiration in a plosive.

References

Abercrombie, D. (1967). *Elements of general phonetics*. Edinburgh University Press.

Abrahamsson, N., & Hyltenstam, K. (2009). Age of onset and nativelikeness in a second language: Listener perception versus linguistic scrutiny. *Language Learning, 52*, 249–306.

Acton, W., Baker, A., Burri, M., & Teaman, B. (2013). Preliminaries to haptic-integrated pronunciation instruction. In J. Levis & K. LeVelle (Eds.), *Proceedings of the 4th pronunciation in second language learning and teaching conference, Aug. 2012* (pp. 234–244). Iowa State University.

Alameen, G., & Levis, J. (2015). Connected speech. In M. Reed & J. Levis (Eds.), *The handbook of English pronunciation* (pp. 159–174). Wiley Blackwell.

Anderson-Hsieh, J., Johnson, R., & Koehler, K. (1992). The relationship between native speaker judgments of nonnative pronunciation and deviance in segmentals, prosody, and syllable structure. *Language Learning, 42*(4), 529–555.

*-Avery, P., & Ehrlich, S. (1992a). Individual sounds of English. In P. Avery & S. Ehrlich (Eds.), *Teaching American English pronunciation* (pp. 11–35). Oxford University Press.

Avery, P., & Ehrlich, S. (1992b). Common pronunciation problems. In P. Avery & S. Ehrlich (Eds.), *Teaching American English pronunciation* (pp. 95–110). Oxford University Press.

Avery, P., & Ehrlich, S. (1992c). Problems of selected language groups. In P. Avery & S. Ehrlich (Eds.), *Teaching American English pronunciation* (pp. 111–160). Oxford University Press.

Baker, A. (2014). Exploring teachers' knowledge of second language pronunciation techniques: Teacher cognitions, observed classroom practices, and student perceptions. *TESOL Quarterly, 48*(1), 136–163.

Beisbier, B. (1995). *Sounds great, Book 2: Intermediate pronunciation and speaking for learners of English*. Thomson Heinle.

Best, C. T. (1995). A direct realist perspective on cross-language speech perception. In W. Strange (Ed.), *Speech perception and linguistic experiences: Theoretical and methodological issues in cross-language speech research* (pp. 167–200). York Press.

Best, C. T., McRoberts, G. W., & Goodell, E. (2001). Discrimination of nonnative consonant contrasts varying in perceptual assimilation to the listener's native phonological system. *Journal of the Acoustical Society of America, 109*(2), 775–794.

Best, C. T., & Tyler, M. D. (2007). Nonnative and second-language speech perception: Commonalities and complementarities. In M. J. Munro & O.-S. Bohn (Eds.), *Language experience in second language speech learning: In honor of James Emil Flege* (pp. 13–34). John Benjamins.

Birdsong, D. (Ed.). (1999). *Second language acquisition and the critical period hypothesis*. Routledge.

Boersma, P., & Weenink, D. (2021). *Praat: Doing phonetics by computer* (Version 6.1.50) (Computer program). Accessed June 20, 2021. www .praat.org.

Bolinger, D. L. M. (1989). *Intonation and its uses: Melody in grammar and discourse*. Stanford University Press.

Brazil, D. (1997). *The communicative value of intonation in English*. Cambridge University Press.

Breitkreutz, J. A., Derwing, T. M., & Rossiter, M. J. (2001). Pronunciation teaching practices in Canada. *TESL Canada Journal, 19*(1), 51–61.

Brown, A. (1988). Functional load and the teaching of pronunciation. *TESOL Quarterly, 22*, 593–606. Also in A. Brown (Ed.). (1991). *Teaching English pronunciation: A book of readings* (pp. 211–224). Routledge.

Brown, A. (Ed.). (1991). *Teaching English pronunciation: A book of readings*. Routledge.

Burri, M., & Baker, A. (2021). 'I feel … slightly out of touch': A longitudinal study of teachers learning to teach English pronunciation over a six-year period. *Applied Linguistics, 42*(4), 791–809. https://doi.org/10.1093/applin/amab009.

Carley, P., & Mees, I. M. (2021). *American English phonetics and pronunciation practice*. Routledge.

Celce-Murcia, M., Brinton, D., & Goodwin, J. (2010). *Teaching pronunciation: A course book and reference guide* (2nd ed.). Cambridge University Press.

Chapman, M. (2007). Theory and practice of teaching discourse intonation. *ELT Journal, 61*(1), 3–11.

Clynes, A., & Deterding, D. (2011). Standard Malay (Brunei). *Journal of the International Phonetic Association, 41*(2), 259–268.

Coe, N. (2001). Speakers of Spanish and Catalan. In M. Swan & B. Smith (Eds.), *Learner English: A teacher's guide to interference and other problems* (pp. 90–112). Cambridge University Press.

Collins, B., & Mees, I. M. (2009). *Practical phonetics and phonology* (2nd ed.). Routledge.

Cooper, R. P., & Aslin, R. N. (1990). Preference for infant-directed speech in the first month after birth. *Child Development, 61*(5), 1584–1595.

Couper, G. (2006). The short- and long-term effects of pronunciation instruction. *Prospect, 21*(1), 46–66.

Couper, G. (2017). Teacher cognition of pronunciation teaching: Teachers' concerns and issues. *TESOL Quarterly, 51*(4), 820–843.

Coxhead, A. (2000). A new academic word list. *TESOL Quarterly, 34*(2), 213–238.

Cruttenden, A. (2014). *Gimson's pronunciation of English* (8th ed.). Routledge.

Crystal, D. (2003). *A dictionary of linguistics & phonetics* (5th ed.). Blackwell.

Cucchiarini, C., Strik, H., & Boves, L. (2000). Different aspects of expert pronunciation quality ratings and their relation to scores produced by speech recognition algorithms. *Speech Communication, 30*(2–3), 109–119.

Cutler, A. (1986). Forbear is a homophone: Lexical prosody does not constrain lexical access. *Language and Speech, 29*(3), 201–220.

Dauer, R. M. (1983). Stress-timing and syllable-timing revisited. *Journal of Phonetics, 21*, 103–108.

Davis, S. (2002). Syllable structure for an artificial language based on universal principles. *Journal of Universal Language, 3*(1), 1–13.

De Bot, K., Lowie, W., & Verspoor, M. (2007). A dynamic systems theory approach to second language acquisition. *Bilingualism, 10*(1), 7–21.

Derwing, T. M., & Munro, M. J. (2005). Second language accent and pronunciation teaching: A research-based approach. *TESOL Quarterly, 39*, 379–397. https://doi.org/10.2307/3588486.

Derwing, T. M., & Munro, M. J. (2015). *Pronunciation fundamentals: Evidence-based perspectives for L2 teaching and research.* John Benjamins.

Derwing, T. M., Munro, M. J., & Wiebe, G. (1998). Evidence in favor of a broad framework for pronunciation instruction. *Language Learning, 48*(3), 393–410.

Derwing, T. M., & Rossiter, M. J. (2003). The effects of pronunciation instruction on the accuracy, fluency, and complexity of L2 accented speech. *Applied Language Learning, 13*(1), 1–17.

Deterding, D. (2006). The pronunciation of English by speakers from China. *English World-Wide, 27*(2), 175–198.

Deterding, D. (2013). *Misunderstandings in English as a lingua franca: An analysis of ELF interactions in south-east Asia.* De Gruyter.

Deterding, D., Wong, J., & Kirkpatrick, A. (2008). The pronunciation of Hong Kong English. *English World-Wide, 29*(2), 148–175.

Ding, S., Liberatore, C., Sonsaat, S., et al. (2019). Golden speaker builder: An interactive tool for pronunciation training. *Speech Communication, 115*, 51–66.

Duanmu, S. (2007). *The phonology of Standard Chinese* (2nd ed.). Oxford.

Ehri, L. C., Nunes, S. R., Stahl, S. A., & Willows, D. M. (2001). Systematic phonics instruction helps students learn to read: Evidence from the National Reading Panel's meta-analysis. *Review of Educational Research, 71*(3), 393–447.

Esling, J. H. (2010). Phonetic notation. In W. J. Hardcastle., J. Laver & F. E. Gibbon (Eds.), *The handbook of phonetic sciences* (pp. 678–702). Wiley Blackwell.

Fernald, A. (1985). Four-month-old infants prefer to listen to motherese. *Infant Behavior and Development, 8*(2), 181–195.

Field, J. (2014). Myth 3: Pronunciation teaching has to establish a set of distinct sounds. In L. Grant (Ed.), *Pronunciation myths: Applying second language research to classroom teaching* (pp. 80–106). University of Michigan Press.

Flege, J. E. (1995). Second language speech learning: Theory, findings, and problems. In W. Strange (Ed.), *Speech perception and linguistic experience: Theoretical and methodological issues in cross-language research* (pp. 233–277). York Press.

Flege, J. E., & Bohn, O.-S. (2021). The revised speech learning model (SLM-r). In R. Wayland (Ed.), *Second language speech learning: Theoretical and empirical progress* (pp. 3–83). Cambridge University Press.

Foote, J. A., Holtby, A. K., & Derwing, T. M. (2011). Survey of the teaching of pronunciation in adult ESL programs in Canada, 2010. *TESL Canada Journal, 29*(1), 1–22.

Fouz-González, J., & Mompean, J. A. (2021). Exploring the potential of phonetic symbols and keywords as labels for perceptual training. *Studies in Second Language Acquisition, 43*(2), 297–328.

Fuchs, R. (2016). *Speech rhythm in varieties of English: Evidence from educated Indian English and British English.* Springer.

Gilbert, J. (2014). Myth 4: Intonation is hard to teach. In L. Grant (Ed.), *Pronunciation myths: Applying second language research to classroom teaching* (pp. 107–136). University of Michigan Press.

Gilbert, J. B. (1991). Gadgets: Non-verbal tools for teaching pronunciation. In A. Brown (Ed.), *Teaching English pronunciation: A book of readings* (pp. 308–322). Routledge.

Gilbert, J. B. (2008). *Teaching pronunciation using the prosody pyramid.* Cambridge University Press.

Gilbert, J. B. (2012). *Clear speech* (4th ed.). Cambridge University Press.

Goh, C. (2000). A cognitive perspective on language learners' listening comprehension problems. *System, 28*(1), 55–75.

Goh, C. (2008). Metacognitive instruction for second language listening development: Theory, practice and research implications. *Regional Language Centre Journal, 39*(2), 188–213.

Grabe, E., & Low E. L. (2002). Durational variability in speech and the rhythm class hypothesis. In C. Gussenhoven & N. Warner (Eds.), *Laboratory phonology 7* (pp. 515–546). Mouton de Gruyter.

Grant, L. (2017). *Well said: Pronunciation for clear communication* (4th ed.). Cengage Learning.

Grosjean, F., & Gee, J. (1987). Prosodic structure and spoken word recognition. *Cognition, 25*, 135–155.

Hahn, L. D. (2004). Primary stress and intelligibility: Research to motivate the teaching of suprasegmentals. *TESOL Quarterly, 38*(2), 201–223.

Hansen, J. G. (2006). *Acquiring a non-native phonology*. Continuum.

Haslam, M. (2018). Teaching the sound system of English. In J. I. Liontas (Ed.), *The TESOL encyclopedia of English language teaching* (pp. 1–7). Wiley Blackwell.

Hayes-Harb, R., & Masuda, K. (2008). Development of the ability to lexically encode novel second language phonemic contrasts. *Second Language Research, 28*, 33–35.

Hieke, A. E. (1987). Absorption and fluency in native and non-native casual speech in English, In A. James and J. Leather (Eds.), *Sound patterns in second language acquisition* (pp. 41–58). Foris.

Hogg, R., & McCully, C. B. (1987). *Metrical phonology: A course book*. Cambridge University Press.

Honikman, B. (1964). Articulatory settings. In D. Abercrombie, D. B. Fry, P. A. D. MacCarthy, N. C. Scott & J. L. M. Trim (Eds.), *In honour of Daniel Jones* (pp. 73–84). Longman.

Howard, I. S., & Messum, P. (2011). Modelling the development of pronunciation in infant speech acquisition. *Motor Control, 15*(1), 85–17.

Hulst, H. van der (2014). *Word stress: Theoretical and typological issues*. Cambridge University Press.

IPA. (1999). *Handbook of the International Phonetic Association: A guide to the use of the International Phonetic Alphabet*. Cambridge University Press.

Jenkins, J. (2000). *The phonology of English as an international language*. Oxford University Press.

Jenkins, J. (2007). *English as a lingua franca: Attitude and identity*. Oxford University Press.

Jones, T. (Ed.). (2016). *Pronunciation in the classroom: The overlooked essential*. TESOL Press.

Jusczyk, P. W., & Derrah, C. (1987). Representation of speech sounds by young infants. *Developmental Psychology, 23*(5), 648–654

Kang, O., Thomson, R. I., & Murphy, J. M. (Eds.). (2018). *The Routledge handbook of contemporary English pronunciation*. Routledge.

Kessler, G. (2018). Technology and the future of language teaching. *Foreign Language Annals, 51*(1), 205–218.

Kissling, E. M. (2013). Teaching pronunciation: Is explicit phonetics instruction beneficial for FL learners? *Modern Language Journal, 97*(3), 720–744.

Koehler, M., & Mishra, P. (2009). What is technological pedagogical content knowledge (TPACK)? *Contemporary Issues in Technology and Teacher Education, 9*(1), 60–70.

Ladd, D. R. (2008). *Intonational phonology*. Cambridge University Press.

Ladefoged, P. (2001). *Vowels and consonants: An introduction to the study of languages*. Blackwell.

Ladefoged, P., & Johnson, K. (2011). *A course in phonetics* (8th ed). Wadsworth Cengage Learning.

Lado, R. (1957). *Linguistics across cultures: Applied linguistics for language teachers*. University of Michigan Press.

Larsen-Freeman, D. (2017). Complexity theory: The lessons continue. In L. Ortega & Z. H. Han (Eds.), *Complexity theory and language development: In celebration of Diane Larsen-Freeman* (pp. 11–50). John Benjamins.

Laver, J. (1994). *Principles of phonetics*. Cambridge University Press.

Lee, J. (2001). Korean speakers. In M. Swan & B. Smith (Eds.), *Learner English: A teacher's guide to interference and other problems* (pp. 325–342). Cambridge University Press.

Lee, J., Jang, J., & Plonsky, L. (2015). The effectiveness of second language pronunciation instruction: A meta-analysis. *Applied Linguistics, 36*(3), 345–366.

Lenneberg, E. (1967). *Biological foundations of language*. Wiley.

Levis, J., & Pickering, L. (2004). Teaching intonation in discourse using speech visualization technology. *System, 32*(4), 505–524.

Levis, J. M. (1999). Intonation in theory and practice, revisited. *TESOL Quarterly, 33*(1), 37–63.

Levis, J. M. (2005). Changing contexts and shifting paradigms in pronunciation teaching. *TESOL Quarterly, 39*(3), 369–377.

Levis, J. M. (2018). *Intelligibility, oral communication, and the teaching of pronunciation*. Cambridge University Press.

Levis, J. M., & Levis, G. M. (2018). Teaching high-value pronunciation features: Contrastive stress for intermediate learners. *CATESOL Journal, 30*(1), 139–160.

Levis, J. M., & Wichmann, A. (2015). English intonation – form and meaning. In M. Reed & J. Levis (Eds.), *The handbook of English pronunciation* (pp. 139–155). Wiley Blackwell.

Lewis, C., & Deterding, D. (2018). Word stress and pronunciation teaching in English as a lingua franca contexts. *CATESOL Journal, 30*(1), 161–176.

Li, X. (2017). The construction of intelligent English teaching model based on artificial intelligence. *International Journal of Emerging Technologies in Learning (iJET), 12*(12), 35–44.

Liu, D., & Reed, M. (2021). Exploring the complexity of the L2 intonation system: An acoustic and eye-tracking study. *Frontiers in Communication, 6*, 627316. https://doi.org/10.3389/fcomm.2021.627316.

Low, E. L., & Brown, A. (2003). *An introduction to Singapore English.* McGraw-Hill.

Low, E. L., Grabe, E., & Nolan, F. (2000). Quantitative characterization of speech rhythm: Syllable-timing in Singapore English. *Language and Speech, 43*(4), 377–401.

Lowie, W., & Bultena, S. (2007). Articulatory settings and the dynamics of second language speech production. In J. Maidman (Ed.), *Proceedings of the Phonetics Teaching and Learning Conference, London.* UCL European Institute.

Lu, X. (2018). Natural language processing and intelligent computer-assisted language learning (ICALL). In J. I. Liontas (Ed.), *The TESOL encyclopedia of English language teaching* (pp. 1–6). Wiley Blackwell.

MacMahon, A. (1996). Phonetic notation. In P. T. Daniels & W. Bright (Eds.), *The world's writing systems* (pp. 821–846). Oxford University Press.

Maddieson, I. (1984). *Patterns of sounds.* Cambridge University Press.

Maddieson, I. (2013). Voicing in plosives and fricatives. In M. S. Dryer & M. Haspelmath (Eds.), *The world atlas of language structures online.* Max Planck Institute for Evolutionary Anthropology. https://wals.info/chapter/4.

McCrocklin, S. (2019). Dictation programs for second language pronunciation learning: Perceptions of the transcript, strategy use and improvement. *Konińskie Studia Językowe, 7*(2), 137–157.

McCrocklin, S., & Edalatishams, I. (2020). Revisiting popular speech recognition software for ESL speech. *TESOL Quarterly, 54*(4), 1086–1097.

McNerney, M., & Mendelsohn, D. (1992). Suprasegmentals in the pronunciation class: Setting priorities. In P. Avery & S. Ehrlich (Eds.), *Teaching American English pronunciation* (pp. 185–196). Oxford University Press.

Mehler, J., Jusczyk, P., Lambertz, G., Halsted, N., Bertoncini, J., & Amiel-Tison, C. (1988). A precursor of language acquisition in young infants. *Cognition, 29*(2), 143–178.

Mendelsohn Burns, I., Avery, P., & Ehrlich, S. (1992). Word stress and vowel reductions. In P. Avery & S. Ehrlich (Eds.), *Teaching American English pronunciation* (pp. 63–72). Oxford University Press.

Messum, P., & Young, R. (2017). Bringing the English articulatory setting into the classroom: (1) the tongue. *Speak Out*, *57*, 29–39.

Miller, S. (2011). Integrating pronunciation into your IEP curriculum. Presented at the TESOL 45th Annual International Convention and Exposition, New Orleans, LA, March 2011.

Mixdorff, H. (2000). A novel approach to the fully automatic extraction of Fujisaki model parameters. In *2000 IEEE International Conference on Acoustics, Speech, and Signal Processing*. Proceedings (Cat. No. 00CH37100) (Vol. 3, pp. 1281–1284). Institute of Electrical and Electronics Engineers.

Mompean, J. A. (2003). Pedagogical tools for teaching articulatory setting. In M. J. Solé & D. Recansens (Eds.), *Proceedings of the 15th International Congress of Phonetic Sciences* (pp. 1603–1606). Causal Productions.

Mompean, J. A. (2017). Doing phonetic transcription in a modern language degree. In J. A. Cutillas Espinosa, J. M. Hernández Campoy, R. M. Manchón Ruiz & F. Mena Martínez (Eds.), *Estudios de Filología Inglesa: Homenaje a D. Rafael Monroy* (pp. 479–505). Editum.

Mompean, J. A., & Fouz-González, J. (2021). Phonetic symbols in contemporary pronunciation instruction. *Regional Language Centre Journal*, *52*(1), 155–168.

Monk, B., & Burak, A. (2001). Russian speakers. In M. Swan & B. Smith (Eds.), *Learner English: A teacher's guide to interference and other problems* (pp. 145–161). Cambridge University Press.

Morett, L. (2014). When hands speak louder than words: The role of gesture in the communication, encoding, and recall of words in a novel second language. *Modern Language Journal*, *98*, 834–853.

Munro, M. J., & Derwing, T. M. (2015). Intelligibility in research and practice. In M. Reed & J. M. Levis (Eds.), *The handbook of English pronunciation* (pp. 375–396). Wiley Blackwell.

Murphy, J. (2014). Myth 7: Teacher training programs provide adequate preparation in how to teach pronunciation. In L. Grant (Ed.), *Pronunciation myths: Applying second language research to classroom teaching* (pp. 188–224). University of Michigan Press.

Murphy, J., & Kandil, M. (2004). Word-level stress patterns in the academic word list. *System*, *32*(1), 61–74.

Nilsen, D. L. F., & Pace Nilsen, A. (2010). *Pronunciation contrasts in English* (2nd ed.). Waveland Press Inc.

Noll, M. (2007). *American accent skills: Vowels and consonants*. The Ameritalk Press.

O'Brien, M. G., Derwing, T. M., Cucchiarini, C., et al. (2018). Directions for the future of technology in pronunciation research and teaching. *Journal of Second Language Pronunciation, 4*(2), 182–207.

O'Connor, J. D., & Arnold, G. F. (1973). *Intonation of colloquial English*. Pearson.

Paunović, T., & Savić, M. (2008). Discourse intonation – Making it work. In S. Komar & U. Mozetič (Eds.), As you write it: Issues in literature, language, and translation in the context of Europe in the 21st century. *English Language Overseas Perspectives and Enquiries, 5*(1–2), 57–75.

Pickering, L. (2006). Current research on intelligibility in English as a lingua franca. *Annual Review of Applied Linguistics, 26*, 219–213.

Pickering, L. (2018). *Discourse intonation: A discourse-pragmatic approach to teaching the pronunciation of English*. University of Michigan Press.

Pierrehumbert, J. B. (1980). *The phonology and phonetics of English intonation* (PhD diss., MIT). Published 1990 by Garland Press.

Pike, K. L. (1945). *The intonation of American English*. University of Michigan Press.

Przedlacka, J. (2018). An overview of phonetics for language teachers. In O. Kang et al. (Eds.), *The Routledge handbook of contemporary English pronunciation* (pp. 40–57). Routledge.

Quam, C., & Swingley, D. (2012). Development in children's interpretation of pitch cues to emotions. *Child Development, 83*(1), 236–250.

Reed, M., & Levis, J. M. (2015). *The handbook of English pronunciation*. Wiley Blackwell.

Reed, M., & Michaud, C. (2015). Intonation in research and practice. In M. Reed & J. Levis (2015). *The handbook of English pronunciation* (pp. 454–470). Wiley Blackwell.

Roach, P. (1982). On the distinction between 'stress-timed' and 'syllable-timed' languages. In D. Crystal (Ed.), *Linguistic controversies* (pp. 73–79). Edward Arnold.

Roach, P. (2009). *English phonetics and phonology* (4th ed.). Cambridge University Press.

Rogerson-Revell, P. (2018). English vowels and consonants. In O. Kang et al. (Eds.), *The Routledge handbook of contemporary English pronunciation* (pp. 93–121). Routledge.

Saito, K. (2007). The influence of explicit phonetic instruction on pronunciation in EFL settings: The case of English vowels and Japanese learners of English. *Linguistics Journal, 2*(3),17–41.

Saito, K. (2012). Effects of instruction on L2 pronunciation development: A synthesis of 15 quasi-experimental intervention studies. *TESOL Quarterly*, *46*(4), 842–854.

Salcedo, C. (2010). The phonological system of Spanish. *Revista de Lingüística y Lenguas Aplicadas*, *5*, 195–209.

Scherling, J. (2012). *Japanizing English: Anglicisms and their impact on Japanese*. Narr Verlag.

Schmidt, R. (2012). Attention, awareness, and individual differences in language learning. In W. M. Chan, K. N. Chin, S. Bhatt & I. Walker (Eds.), *Perspectives on individual characteristics and foreign language education* (pp. 27–50). De Gruyter Mouton.

Schwaber, K., & Beedle, M. (2002). *Agile software development with Scrum*. Prentice Hall.

Seidlhofer, B. (2011). *Understanding English as a lingua franca*. Oxford University Press.

Selinker, L. (1972). Interlanguage. *International Review of Applied Linguistics*, *10*(1–4), 209–232. https://doi.org/10.1515/iral.1972.10.1-4.209.

Smith, B. (2001). Arabic speakers. In M. Swan & B. Smith (Eds.), *Learner English: A teacher's guide to interference and other problems* (pp. 195–213). Cambridge University Press.

Smyth, D. (2001). Thai speakers. In M. Swan & B. Smith (Eds.), *Learner English: A teacher's guide to interference and other problems* (pp. 343–356). Cambridge University Press.

Stone, M. (2010). Laboratory techniques for investigating speech articulation. In W. J. Hardcastle, J. Laver & F. E. Gibbon (Eds.), *The handbook of phonetic sciences* (2nd ed.) (pp. 9–38). Wiley Blackwell.

Swan, M., & Smith, B. (Eds.). (2001). *Learner English: A teacher's guide to interference and other problems*. Cambridge University Press.

Taylor, K., & Thompson, S. (2015). Color vowel™ chart (4th ed.). English Language Training Solutions. https://learn.colorvowel.com/.

Taylor, K., & Thompson, S., & R. Barr. (2016). *The color vowel approach: Resources for connecting spoken English to vocabulary, reading, and spelling*. English Language Training Solutions.

Thomson, R. I. (2018). High variability [pronunciation] training (HVPT): A proven technique about which every language teacher and learner ought to know. *Journal of Second Language Pronunciation*, *4*(2), 208–231.

Thomson, R. I., & Derwing, T. M. (2015). The effectiveness of L2 pronunciation instruction: A narrative review. *Applied Linguistics*, *36*(3), 326–344.

Tsunemoto, A., Trofimovich, P., & Kennedy, S. (2020). Pre-service teachers' beliefs about second language pronunciation teaching, their experience, and speech assessments. *Language Teaching Research*. https://doi.org/10.1177/1362168820937273.

Vandergrift, L., & Goh, C. (2012). *Teaching and learning second language listening: Metacognition in action*. Routledge.

Vihman, M. (1993). Variable paths to early word production. *Journal of Phonetics, 21*, 61–82.

Vihman, M. (2014). *Phonological development: The first two years* (2nd ed.). Wiley Blackwell.

Walker, R. (2010). *Teaching the pronunciation of English as a lingua franca*. Oxford.

Waninge, F., De Bot, K., & Dörnyei, Z. (2014). Motivational dynamics in second language learning: Change, stability and context. *Modern Language Journal, 98*, 704–723.

Wells, J. C. (1982). *Accents of English*. Cambridge University Press.

Wells, J. C. (2006). *English intonation: An introduction*. Cambridge University Press.

Wen, Z., Biedron, A., & Skehan, P. (2016). Foreign language aptitude theory: Yesterday, today, and tomorrow. *Language Teaching, 50*, 1–31.

Wennerstrom, A. (2001). *The music of everyday speech*. Oxford University Press.

Werker, J. F., & Tees, R. C. (1983). Developmental changes across childhood in the perception of non-native speech sounds. *Canadian Journal of Psychology/Revue canadienne de psychologie, 37*(2), 278–286.

Wichmann, A. (2005). *Intonation in text and discourse*. Longman.

Xu, Y. (2004). Transmitting tone and intonation simultaneously – the parallel encoding and target approximation (PENTA) model. In *Proceedings of international symposium on tonal aspects of languages: With emphasis on tone languages* (pp. 215–220).

Yong, J. Y. (2001). Malay/Indonesian speakers. In M. Swan & B. Smith (Eds.), *Learner English: A teacher's guide to interference and other problems* (pp. 279–295). Cambridge University Press.

Zielinski, B. (2015). The segmental/suprasegmental debate. In M. Reed & J. Levis (Eds.), *The handbook of English pronunciation* (pp. 397–412). Wiley Blackwell.

Zielinski, B., & Yates, L. (2014). Myth 2: Pronunciation instruction is not appropriate for beginning-level learners. In L. Grant (Ed.), *Pronunciation myths: Applying second language research to classroom teaching* (pp. 56–79). University of Michigan Press.

Cambridge Elements ☰

Phonetics

Elements in the Series

Printed in the United States
by Baker & Taylor Publisher Services